Wildlife's Christmas Treasury

Library of Congress **CIP** Data: page 159

White-tailed deer forage for food in a snowstorm.

Wildlife's Christmas Treasury

NATIONAL
WILDLIFE
FEDERATION

Contents

*Scarlet leaves surrounding tiny blossoms
make the poinsettia a Christmas favorite.*

Reflections on Winter

In winter the pulse of the earth slows down. In the mountains, fields and woods, a hush falls over the land. Crickets have ceased to fiddle, bees no longer invade the meadow, and the frogs' serenade stopped months ago. The woodchuck has disappeared to sleep away the night-drenched days, and the noisy chipmunk has hurried into the den he claimed for himself to nap. The yellow-breasted chat, the rose-breasted grosbeak, the purple martin, and the oriole have all fled far south to enjoy December's summer in a distant land. At first glance all the world seems deserted.

But look and listen closely. The earth is alive. The deer wanders restlessly, browsing on twigs of willow and alder; and paws the snow to claim an acorn buried in the dirt, an ear of corn left lying in the field. The porcupine gnaws eagerly on hemlock and pine, and the beaver enjoys his cache of birch and aspen, set aside for winter snacking. The otter toboggans across snowy hills in search of food and fun. The fox prowls the land, barking his pleasure, and the coyote sings his mournful song. There's that chipmunk, poking his nose out again at the first sniff of a thaw, determined not to miss a bit of sun.

A titmouse perches on a berry-laden shrub and goldfinches flock to the feeder. Rejoice in an ounce of chickadee resting lightly in a pine tree and in juncos, pecking in the snow. Listen for ice heaving on the pond, and frozen puddles cracking under foot; and listen for wide-eyed owls hooting in the night. Look closely and you'll see buds ripe with the promise of next year's spring, and holly signaling this year's Christmas. For the earth, stripped bare by winter, is still teeming with life waiting to be seen and heard.

This is the season for poetry, story and song to declare our wonder . . . and our amusement . . . and our love of wildlife. In woodcut and photograph, in painting and toy, in legend and myth, we declare it, for without these wonders of nature the earth is truly still, not just muted for a season. These are our Christmas treasures . . . all that nature has given.

The reflection of Oregon's Mt. Hood floats serenely on the waters of Lost Lake.

December Days

There is a special kind of magic in a cold December landscape, missing at other times of the year. In December—the year's finale —the very world about us seems to be encircled in a large, transparent bubble.

Confetti-like snow swirls down from heaven to blanket the ground. A kaleidoscope of beauty assaults us: the sparkling breath of frost on a spider's web; an overgrown meadow with browning clumps of orchard grass; a sad stalk of thistle bent by determined winds; the sculptured hollow of a seedless pod; the stillness of a stream silenced by ice.

Suddenly, we awake to the sound of a scolding jay as it flies overhead. Nature has ways of letting us know that we are never truly alone—not even on a cold and private day in the month of December.

Freezing temperatures bring snow—winter's imprint—to this icy creek in the Colorado Rockies, near Vail.

9

Christmas Across the Land

Drawing a profile of our nation at Christmas is almost impossible, for the continental U.S. alone stretches through some 25 degrees of latitude, 15,000 feet of altitude, and more than 100 degrees of temperature from the bathing beaches of Key West to the ice-fishing shanties of Minnesota.

To present America at Christmas we turned, therefore, to five photographers and five conservation journalists, in the five corners of the lower 48 states, and asked them to take us on a Christmas walk through their favorite winter places. Even without Alaska or Hawaii, the contrasts are great and the similarities are striking.

Castle Rock looms above Arizona's Oak Creek Canyon.

The Southwestern winter

is full of contrasts—warm deserts and high, cold forests; arid mesas and sparkling lakes and streams; bustling cities and ghost towns. Wildlife here, however, offers less seasonal contrast than any other part of the country.

A Christmas walk will find all the familiar wildlife neighbors—deer, jackrabbits, doves, quail, ground squirrels, 'coons and skunks—right at home, for their summer and winter homes are at the same addresses. We'll find the white-winged doves gone or going at Christmas, though, and northern waterfowl of all kinds settling down in their winter places for variety, but otherwise, the habitats show more contrast than the winter wildlife—from New Mexico missile ranges to Los Angeles suburbs.

Our first problem, unique to my area, is that a Christmas walk can go to—or through—as many as seven different life zones in a few miles. We'll have to decide which to visit to be sure to see a real sample of the Southwest at Christmas. In the lower elevations and desert in the winter, we can find both human and wild residents enjoying the moderate daytime temperatures—even welcoming the occasional dusting of snow that frosts the sun-burned rocks.

But if we move a thousand feet higher up the nearby slope, we find the desert giving way to low mountains and lush grasslands, with bighorn sheep, coyotes, cougars, and such exotics as the ring-tail cat and comical coatimundi. Higher, at the 5,000-foot level, we'll see snow, with antelope, bears, turkeys, band-tail pigeons, and trout. Still higher, we'll find ponderosa pines standing in deep snow —and elk!

So to the Southwesterner, the question of a Christmas hike may not be "shall we?", but "where?". This striking cross-section of topography, climate, plant life and wildlife guarantees something to please the eye of any nature lover, from endless marching sand dunes and "forests" of towering saguaro cactus to deep pine and juniper forests, wrapped in snow most of the winter months and displayed against moonscape shapes of rugged mountains.

The coolness, the silence, the color and life of the Southwest will reward our Christmas hike wherever we go.

Bob Schimmel

Canada geese search for food in a Massachusetts pond.

If you're coming with me

for a Christmas walk somewhere in the Northeast, with our snow and cold, you'll need a solid foundation. So, I'd recommend you get a good breakfast in you, before we begin. In Vermont it's most likely to be wheat cakes with maple syrup. We'll take along a couple of Baldwin apples with us, although in midmorning it will be like biting into a snowball to taste them.

But we must move along if we're going to get anywhere before the sun is full out. We're starting out from my favorite place, a pre-Revolutionary village in southern Vermont, on the first rise of hills into the Green Mountains. On the main street, surrounded by lawns and white colonial houses, atop a granite base is a life-size bronze statue of a catamount—cougar to you, possibly. It isn't likely that we will encounter one, but periodically there are unconfirmed reports of the living beast, both in Vermont and New York. But as you step out with me along the main road, the biggest animal you'll see right close is a lonely gray squirrel hopping among the row of sugar maples.

But let's cut through a cornfield, toward the higher ground. A hundred yards away you see a movement of red, white and bronze among the cornstalks —a cock pheasant, an uncommon sight in Vermont. With him is a drab hen. They walk away alertly, but strangely unafraid. You go along upwards and into the first low balsam and Scotch pine, treading softly, for this is white-tailed deer country. Then ten yards away there is a blast of noise and wings, and a partridge takes off. You find there is an old abandoned apple tree among the conifers and trudge over to see what else may have been feeding there. And, sure enough, there was another, a doe, shown by her tracks. At one place you could see she had reared high on her hind legs to reach one remaining apple in the tree.

Trailed by yammering blue jays, you finally reach your destination, a summer camp among the big balsam near the summit of the hill. You can look out over the valley here, before starting back, and the fragrance of the balsam needles enters your lungs, and you wonder if that is why you feel so whole.

Jim Gavagan

13

Table Mountain in Washington's Mount Baker National Forest.

You'll have to fly with me

to travel over this favored land, my Pacific Northwest, this Christmas. But why not? That way, our giant strides can stay in scale with the vastness of Nature's remarkable bounty.

The first long rays of the Christmas morning sun stream through the high passes, around the jagged peaks of the Continental Divide below us. The thick stillness of precious snow lies in fields of solid white everywhere.

Leaving the Rockies, we follow the sun and the thinning snow onto the broad flatlands of the Columbia Plateau.

The tiny silver fingers against the mountain face below us are the beginnings of the mighty Columbia River System, the lifeblood of the Northwest. These tiny threads join others, over thousands of miles of watersheds. As we watch, they become the Clark Fork and Kootenai in the north; the Spokane, Coeur d'Alene, Saint Joe, Clearwater, Salmon and Snake in the center; the Yakima, John Day, Deschutes and Willamette from the south.

Coastal streams pour their life-giving wealth down the western slopes of the Cascades, providing highways for salmon migrating inland to spawn.

As we look down over this beautiful and dynamic scene of natural grandeur and resources, we might pause and reflect on its future. How long will those virgin slopes of timber and clear, silver waters remain as God's blessing on those who inhabit this favored part of earth?

Conservation has been a struggle. Man's use of the best parts of this land has left brutal scars on the face of it.

The great chinook salmon once migrated up the Columbia and its tributaries by the millions. Today the remnants are counted in thousands.

Antelope roamed much of the region; now isolated bands are carefully nurtured with every technique of modern wildlife management. The remaining buffalo live on refuges. We are grateful, at least, that our efforts to conserve and protect have made their mark.

As we step down from our tour, we realize that we could not begin to describe winter in the Northwest—it is too much. We are only thankful that we can be here and see it this Christmas Day.

Marshall Edson

The Southeast abounds

with wildlife in winter, so a Christmas walk can be a panorama of so many creatures that you'll forget the lack of picturesque—uncomfortable—ice and snow.

The *kuk-kuk-kuk-kukkuk* of the pileated woodpecker, perched on the side of the majestic oak, greets us as we walk the sun-drenched hardwood bottomland.

Stephen—Tommy—see those five wood ducks go. Hear them chatter: *hoo-eek! hoo-eek!* They'll glide into that pin oak flat just up ahead. Yes, it's Christmas Morn but there's none of that white stuff on the ground here. Just fallen leaves, soft from dew.

Listen to the blue jays. They'll probably continue to fly just ahead of us. Noisy rascals! Watch our other wild friends scatter, now, through the forest.

Marcile—Peggy—look over there to the left. A huge briar patch. Big, fat old Br'er Rabbit may scamper out of there anytime, and surprise you.

Let's stay on the trail now. Look—that little gray squirrel over there. He's scratching for those "puckons" he hid last October.

Come on, you all, we've still a lot of territory to cover. Look over yonder, Murry. That old mama possum has just come out of her den. Up north, she wouldn't dare venture out this early—if at all. She hates the cold.

Haven't seen a deer track all morning. That's unusual, too. Hunters have been running dogs in this here cut all season. Look over that palmetto ridge. You may get to see that big wild turkey gobbler you been talking about, Peggy.

Now, hustle along, Marcile and Jay. There goes that old doe. Likely as not a big buck is nearby. Look, she's stopped—just a hundred yards from us. She may have a fawn hiding in that brush heap over to your left.

Why not circle back over to that hidden lake. We may get to see some redheads yet.

Ho! You hear 'em . . . Pintails! There must be fifteen in that bunch. They are called "sprigtails" in the East. They're going down. Right in our old blind.

It's a wonderful day. And that turkey dinner, yet to come. There's the car over there. Look back one more time. Beauty, beauty everywhere—and peace.

Steve Harmon

Snow geese above marsh at Pea Island, North Carolina.

White-tailed deer—alert beside Minnesota's Lake Superior.

Winter in the north woods

is really *winter*, so you'll need these snowshoes for a hike in the northern Midwest. Even foot-deep snow is tiring without them, and anyway, our webbed wake will be more interesting to look back on than boot tracks.

Those chickadees. Chances are they'll be our companions all the way. You wonder if they aren't on some kind of assignment to keep our whereabouts a matter of common knowledge among the other creatures. Nevertheless, they're friendly little companions.

See that little blowout in the snow just ahead of us, with no tracks around it? That's where a grouse burst into flight from his self-heated shelter.

We'll stay close to this creek now. There's a beaver pond not far from here. . . . Wouldn't it be a thrill to take a trout out of that black water and land him in this soft snow?

Those little tracks on our left. A gray or red squirrel made them. You can see where he did some acorn searching.

Yes, there's the beaver pond. Not much evidence of their being busy, though. Christmas time is beaver vacation time, I guess.

Now we'll veer off a bit to our left and visit a deeryard. It's just over the ridge . . . . No, a dog didn't make those tracks. They were made by a fox, raiding the icebox for a midnight mouse.

Yes, down there is the deeryard. This one covers about 200 acres, I'm told. It's a popular one with the white-tails, and much used every winter. This time of the year, dense evergreens provide shelter.

We'll walk into the deeryard a short way to give you an idea of how protective these dense conifers can be. Takes quite a wind to penetrate, and without wind the cold loses much of its sting. There —there, just ahead of us—that buck is watching our every move.

Don't look back yet—not until we reach the top of the ridge. I want to save the view we're about to enjoy for the climax to our hike.

Did you ever see a Christmas card half so beautiful?

And the stillness. That seems beautiful in its own way too.

I'm sure we both agree—there is peace on earth, after all.

John Gray

Dashing through the snow

Currier and his wife, in a favorite Currier and Ives print.

in a two horse open sleigh!

Allegro.

PIANO

1. Dashing thro' the snow, In a one horse open sleigh, — O'er the hills we
2. A day or two a-go I thought I'd take a ride, And soon Miss Fan-nie

go, — Laughing all the way; Bells on bob tail ring, — Making spirits
Bright Was seat-ed by my side, The horse was lean and lank; Mis-for-tune seemd his

bright, — Oh what sport to ride and sing A sleighing song to night.
lot. He got in-to a drift-ed bank, And we, we got up-set.

CHORUS.

SOP. Jingle bells, Jingle bells, Jingle all the way; Oh! what joy it

ALTO

TENOR Jingle bells, Jingle bells, Jingle all the way; Oh! what joy it

BASS

Piano

20

Jingle Bells, filled with the pleasures of a snowy world, is a song that we traditionally associate with winter and more especially with Christmas. Written in 1857 by James Pierpont, a Unitarian minister, the song was created for Sunday-school entertainment.

The magic of snow has been drawing children and adults alike out-of-doors for centuries—in horse-drawn sleigh, on skis, or afoot. On the preceding page, a print shows Nathaniel Currier and his wife enjoying a ride in their open sleigh with horses trotting and bells jingling, and all at once Pierpont's words and music spring to life. The original drawing was a personal gift to Currier from the employees of the little New York print shop of N. Currier—destined to become the Currier & Ives firm in 1857. Among the estimated 7,000 litho-graphs turned out by the shop over a 70 year period are many others depicting the "glories" of winter. These, not surprisingly, have be-come Christmas card classics.

3.

A day or two ago,
The story I must tell
I went out on the snow
And on my back I fell;
A gent was riding by
In a one horse open sleigh,
He laughed as there I sprawling lie,
But quickly drove away.

4.

Now the ground is white
Go it while you're young,
Take the girls to night
And sing this sleighing song;
Just get a bob tailed bay
Two forty as his speed
Hitch him to an open sleigh
And crack, you'll take the lead.

Winter's Secrets

There are sounds in the sky when the
*   year grows old,*
And the winds of the winter blow—
When night and the moon are clear and cold,
And the stars shine on the snow;
Or wild is the blast and the bitter sleet
That beats on the window pane.
But blest on the frosty hills are the feet
Of the Christmas time again!
Chiming sweet when the night wind swells,
Blest is the sound of the Christmas Bells!

Author Unknown

Far removed from the everyday bustle of urban life, a tranquilizing calm dominates this snow scene in West Virginia's Cathedral State Park. Because it protects a rare stand of virgin timber, the park is a Registered Natural Landmark.

Four Paintings by the Artist

This morning I saw through my window the first idle flakes of the year's first real snow. Small, scattered, and casual, they might have passed almost unnoticed. But it is thus that great things begin, and to a practiced eye they had the air of meaning business.

They were not fluffy like the playful flakes of a precocious flurry, nor wet like the end-of-the-season falls, which turn first to sleet and then to rain. Instead, they were the single, hard, sparkling little crystals which look as though they intended to remain just that, and come down with quiet confidence, as though they knew they are merely the advance guard of many to follow and to support them. The first tender green of April is not more deceptively tentative, more unspectacular in appearance. Neither is it surer of itself. Equally, the first green and the first white seem to say, "I know that my time has come. It is now that I shall inherit the earth."

Such things as this one never quite remembers. One recognizes them when they appear again, as one recognizes the opening bars of a symphony one could not whistle or hum. What is to follow is not so much recalled as prepared for, and it will magically combine the charm of the familiar with the charm of the new. Memory can never reconstruct for itself the infinite, felicitous detail. Winter, like spring and like Mozart, is always richer and more varied than one remembered it.

I have, when I care to look back at them, my charts and my tables. On the graph of the daily maxima and minima recorded by my thermometer, the coming of winter means two irregular lines which erratically rise and fall while they tend ever downward. In my diary it means, less nakedly, a series of visible phenomena, from the blazing of the dying leaves to the hardening of the ground and the gradual fading of color, until blackness and whiteness come to dominate. But no sum of such details will

Each season newly decorates the landscape. On this and the two succeeding pages, a single New Jersey pond scene is captured in winter, spring, summer, and fall.

add up to any adequate account of what has been happening. . . .

Any analogy with winter dooms us to choose a lesser thing for comparison with that which we intend to exalt. What is now about to begin Thoreau grandly denominated "that grand old poem called Winter." One is not likely to better him when he is, as here, at his best. And yet even a poem is not really so complex a thing as this winter which operates not only upon the mind, but upon all the senses as well, and which one does not merely contemplate because one is also a part of it. Perhaps it is a poem, . . . but it is also a drama, a symphony, and a picture.

Some small part of the drama is visible even from a box seat in front of a window through which one may catch glimpses of birds and beasts whose existence is affected far more drastically than ours, and one may guess also at what is going on below the surface of the snow; below even the surface of soil, where innumerable creatures are sleeping—almost as deeply as the very tree roots—a sleep from which some will awaken, but which, for some others, will pass into imperceptible death. That same window may become also a picture frame, though it is the frame of a picture which changes as no painted picture can, a picture which passes through a series of modulations, each in itself as beautiful as though it were a final end—to become successively the picture of summer, the picture of autumn, and finally the picture of winter.

The very style of the artist seems to change, as he gives his allegiance to one school after another. In summer he was all for Dutch or German minuteness. He cluttered his canvas with detail; affected on a perhaps unsuitably large scale the methods of the miniaturist. As autumn came, he began to simplify, to go in for broader, bolder effects, and then, as the snow came, he realized the impressiveness of large areas and large masses. At last, when everything except the largest features of any landscape has been buried, he becomes almost an abstractionist. There seems nothing left to paint except an idea.

But one is not compelled to remain always standing before the picture frame, or confined to the spectator's side of the proscenium. One may walk into the picture, become part of the poem, or even participate in the drama itself. From no mere canvas does the wind actually blow; there is no poem from which a snowflake can detach itself to melt upon the cheek. From every man-made poem, or picture, or drama, one is to some extent excluded. A certain separateness from it is necessary if it is to be art at all. We must contemplate and we must not intervene. But of nature's poems and pictures we are invited to become a part. This winter which is just coming in offers the detachment of an aesthetic experience, combined with the immediacy of living. . . .

Joseph Wood Krutch

Frost Flowers

Fragile winter dreams in ice,
sparkling thistledown,
and frosted stars
tremble in the morning light,
melt, and freeze anew.

—Candida Palmer

That first real snow inadequately celebrated in the preceding chapter was soon followed by a second. Over the radio the weatherman talked lengthily about cold masses and warm masses, about what was moving out to sea and what wasn't. . . . From my stationary position the most reasonable explanation seemed to be simply that winter had not quite liked the looks of the landscape as she first made it up. . . .

Another forty-eight hours brought one of those nights ideal for frosting the panes. When I came down to breakfast, two of the windows were almost opaque and the others were etched with graceful, fernlike sprays of ice which looked rather like the impressions left in rocks by some of the antediluvian plants, and they were almost as beautiful as anything which the living can achieve. Nothing else which has never lived looks so much as though it were actually informed with life. . . .

Indoors it so happened that a Christmas cactus had chosen this moment to bloom. Its lush blossoms, fuchsia-shaped but pure red rather than magenta, hung at the drooping ends of strange, thick stems and outlined themselves in blood against the glistening background of the frosty pane—jungle flower against frost flower; the warm beauty that breathes and lives and dies competing with the cold beauty that burgeons, not because it wants to, but merely because it is obeying the laws of physics which require that crystals shall take the shape they have always taken since the world began. The effect of red flower against white tracery was almost too theatrical, not quite in good taste perhaps. My eye recoiled in shock and sought through a clear area of the glass the more normal out-of-doors.

On the snowcapped summit of my bird-feeder a chickadee pecked at the newfallen snow and swallowed a few of the flakes which serve him in lieu of the water he sometimes sadly lacks when there is nothing except ice too solid to be picked at. A downy woodpecker was hammering at a lump of suet. . . .

But I soon realized that at the moment the frosted windows were what interested me most—especially the fact that there is no other natural phenomenon in which the lifeless mocks so closely the living. One might almost think that the frost flower had got the idea from the leaf and the branch if one did not know how inconceivably more ancient the first is. . . .

No man ever saw a dinosaur. The last of these giant reptiles was dead eons before the most dubious half-man surveyed the world about him. Not even the dinosaurs ever cast their dim eyes upon many of the still earlier creatures which preceded them. Life changes so rapidly that its later phases know nothing of those which preceded them. But the frost flower is older than the dinosaur, older than the protozoan, older no doubt than the enzyme or the ferment. Yet it is precisely what it has always been. Millions of years before there were any eyes to see it, millions of years before any life existed, it grew in its own special way, crystallized along its preordained lines of cleavage, stretched out its pseudo-branches and pseudo-leaves. It was beautiful before beauty itself existed. . . .

"Life," so the platitudinarian is fond of saying, "is strange." But from our standpoint it is not really so strange as those things which have no life and yet nevertheless move in their predestined orbits and "act". . . .

The snowflake eternally obeys its one and only law: "Be thou six pointed"; the planets their one and only: "Travel thou in an ellipse." The astronomer can tell where the North Star will be ten thousand years hence; the botanist cannot tell where the dandelion will bloom tomorrow.

Life is rebellious and anarchical, always testing the supposed immutability of the rules which the nonliving changelessly accepts. Because the snowflake goes on doing as it was told, its story up to the end of time was finished when it first assumed the form which it has kept ever since. But the story of every living thing is still in the telling. It may hope and it may try. Moreover, though it may succeed or fail, it will certainly change. No form of frost flower ever became extinct. Such, if you like, is its glory. But such also is the fact which makes it alien. It may melt but it cannot die. . . .

While I slept the graceful pseudo-fronds crept across the glass, assuming, as life itself does, an intricate organization. "Why live," they seem to say, "when we can be beautiful, complicated, and orderly without the uncertainty and effort required of a living thing? Once we were all that was. Perhaps some day we shall be all that is. Why not join us?"

Last summer no clod or no stone would have been heard if it had asked such a question. The hundreds of things which walked and sang, the millions which crawled and twined were all having their day. What was dead seemed to exist only in order that the living might live upon it. The plants were busy turning the inorganic into green life and the animals were busy turning that green into red. When we moved, we walked mostly upon grass. Our pre-eminence was unchallenged.

On this winter day nothing seems so successful as the frost flower. It thrives on the very thing which has driven some of us indoors or underground and which has been fatal to many. It is having now its hour of triumph. . . .

I need, so I am told, a faith, something outside myself to which I can be loyal . . . and I know, though vaguely, what I think that is. Wordsworth's God had his dwelling in the light of setting suns. But the God who dwells there seems to be most probably the God of the atom, the star, and the crystal. Mine, if I have one, reveals Himself in another class of phenomena. He makes the grass green and the blood red.

Joseph Wood Krutch

𝒜rriving silently when nights are cold and humid, the magic of frost turns an ordinary landscape into a world of burnished silver. Frost is born as the invisible water in the atmosphere touches lightly on grass, leaf, and windowpane cold enough to freeze it. Lasting only until the sun melts it, frost briefly holds the water vapor captive in a lacy mantle.

Frost, this special gift of the darkness, may be columnar *in shape, composed of minute hollow tubes of ice crystals, or it may be* tabular, *resembling snowflakes. But rarely will these two forms occur on the same night.*

In the autumn, frost comes as nature's harbinger—serving notice that the snows of winter are not far away.

Tracings of columnar frost highlighting blades of grass.

Queen Anne's Lace adorned with frost.

Hoarfrost sparkling on a stem of winterberry.

Autumn's morning glaze on blueberry leaves.

Glitter of frost on an abandoned nest.

On this page, clockwise: *blue spruce cone awaiting spring; weed sentinels on guard; ice-encrusted poverty grass; milkweed pod adorned by crystalline tears; catkins and leaf of the white birch in winter's encasement.*

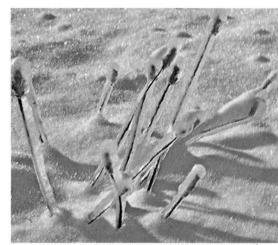

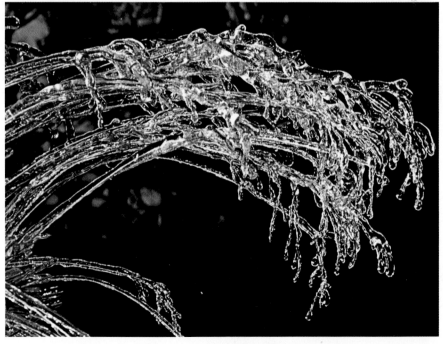

Reading from top left: a pine mohonk's winter bouquet; swordlike blades of grass; cattails scattered like pick-up sticks; salute from the cranberry viburnum; pitch pine trumpets proclaiming Christmas.

Snow Fantasies

*" There they lie, like the wreck of chariot
wheels after a battle in the skies . . . these
glorious spangles, the sweepings of
heaven's floor. And they sing, melting as
they sing, of the mysteries of the
number six, six, six, six."*

—Henry David Thoreau

A garland of ice crystals, immortalized by the camera, frames
the soft, cold beauty that is Yosemite in winter.

The photographs surrounding the Yosemite scene were made
by P. G. Hoff, a Chicago weatherman, who captured each snowflake individually on a glass slide, covered it with clear plastic,
and then stored it in a freezer. The pictures were later taken
through a microscope, under colored lights.

Snow Free

It began at night as a gentle tapping at the windows, long, spectral white fingers of snow lulling us to sleep at bedtime. When we awakened in the morning the fingers had clenched into a giant white fist clouting the countryside. The radio was bleating warnings, roads and schools closing, entire rural communities snowbound. The storm had unexpectedly swerved in from the sea to the south, dumping fast-mounting snow.

My wife and I watched anxiously as the downfall increased, the flakes now the size of nickels, pulling a white screen down firmly over our world. All day, vision through our windows was blocked, giving us the feeling of huddling in a cave, an instant throwback on evolution, frightening with its elemental message: If the storm continued with this force we would soon be stranded.

Our nearest neighbor was over a half-mile away, our driveway a quarter-mile long. I decided to walk to the garage 200 yards from the house to survey the situation. I didn't make it. By the time I had walked 50 feet the snow had knitted a heavy overcoat around me that nearly sent me to my knees. This was killer snow, wet, heavy, blinding, sticky.

At dusk it was still falling. Over coffee, we sat at the kitchen table and assessed. I am a kidney-stone builder, had one surgically removed last year and had been warned that even with diet such is the mysterious chemistry of the body that one never knows when another stone will appear. Lately I'd had several warning twinges. Doctors told me that an unpassed stone causes the third most violent pain known to man. I consider it the first. What if I had to get out suddenly as I did last year? "How would we make it?" worried my wife.

What I was secretly fearing the most now happened. This was snow with the weight of wet sand. The telephone trilled like a dying bird and conked out, the lights went, then the furnace clanked to a halt.

But nothing happened to the snow. It kept coming, a mute, merciless force. I sent up a prayer of thanks for our little take-over generator with its 50-gallon tank of gas that could give us light and heat—if it worked. I heard it faintly sputter in its shed out there in the storm, die out, sputter again, die out. We both sat turned to stone. Then it took over with a gentle faraway purr, the most pleasant sound we'd ever heard.

But we had to be careful. "Use only essential lights, no unnecessary electrical equipment," the directions stated when we had the generator installed last year. The point was to keep heat in the house, prevent the water from freezing, the pipes from bursting, have enough power for lights and cooking. Nothing else. So out came the TV plug and everything else that in this emergency became excess civilized junk—floor lamps, toaster, electric can opener, mixers.

Luckily our fireplace baskets were full, so we put on sweaters, built a fire and turned the thermostat to 50 so the furnace wouldn't siphon off too much of the generator's power.

I turned on our transistor radio. A mistake. Freak February storm . . . Worst in a decade . . . 60 mile-an-hour gale force winds, reaching 100 miles in places . . . Twenty dead so far . . . Tides rising 12 feet above normal, causing evacuation of seaside communities . . . Power failures, roads blocked all over our state of Connecticut . . . more than 20 inches of snow fell yesterday, expected to exceed that today . . . I snapped the radio off.

And we had other problems: My wife's father was seriously ill and the telephone was our instant contact. I was due in New York City tomorrow. A novel I had spent three years writing had gone sour. My publisher had decided that it was far from right. Something to do with my lack of compassion for three secondary characters and an unsympathetic cockiness to my main character, my agent told me. If we couldn't work it out, three years of work might go down the drain. I hadn't been looking forward to the meeting, for I disagreed. But it was imperative that I be there.

The snow fell like a white tide from the sky to envelop the house. Long, glistening pendants of ice grew—in window's view—as the melting water from the roof stretched earthward and froze.

"There's nothing we can do about it," my wife said, knowing I was upset. "Everyone on the East Coast knows about the blizzard by now. There really is no point in worrying. Let's just live it out the best we can."

Without the usual television, the house stood silent and strange. The fire talked to us from the fireplace, logs crackling in laughter, sighing as they fell into embers. Our Siamese cats, Shan and Thai, followed us about as if tied to us with a string, looking up to see if everything was all right. Normal procedure was disturbed and cats dislike any break in routine. Now I thought about normal procedure. How did it go?

After work, it seemed to be built around a drink before dinner—and television. News, sports, weather, favorite programs. All-enveloping. Then tidying up the kitchen and bed. I remembered suddenly that the cats didn't like TV, disappearing almost as soon as we snapped it on. They were sweet cats, we told each other now, absolutely perfect companions, and we hadn't been doing right by them.

Shan and Thai purring on our laps before the fire, we sat talking, chatting like children with so many things to say that they said it all too quickly. We both stopped, laughing. "You know, Jack, this is the first we've *really* talked in years," my wife said, serious now. "Civilization is turning us into robots."

I stared at her. She was right. We used to have so much to talk about. What had happened? With the wind howling at our windows, we sat making a big deal out of dinner. We would use our camp stove, the bottled butane gas, in order to conserve electricity, and make a French stew from four lamb chops we were going to cook hurriedly. I remembered we had three small turnips, some white onions and carrots. My wife left the room and came waltzing back with a bottle of red burgundy wine in her hands, the firelight making it shine like a great ruby. "I just remembered!" she said. "This was stowed away when your editor didn't come last month."

I thought of an old poet's line, took the flashing bottle from her, bowed and held it out. "And all the world a ruby for your finger ring," I quoted. The cats stared as if we had gone mad. Two creatures who usually sat placid in chairs, silently staring for hours at a flickering white light in a box, had suddenly come to life and they didn't know what to make of it. My wife remembered two other times that we had been cut off from the world, once on a boat, another time on a small island. "It was wonderful," she said, "but then we had ship-to-shore radio on the boat, and a telephone on the island."

Real conversation began. Stoking up the little camp stove with its gas cylinder, we put the stew to simmering, added wine and poured ourselves a glass smooth as velvet . . . then went back to the cats and the fire. My wife, looking me in the eye, told me that she agreed with my publisher about the novel. "It isn't *you*, Jack," she said. "I never seemed to have the chance to tell you before. It seems like you're holding back. Those aren't your people in the book. They're somebody else's."

She talked as she hadn't in years, making me realize again what an unusual and perceptive person she was. By the time dinner was finished, eaten before the fire—for us a lamb tastier than any *navarin* dished out by the finest French restaurant—she had solved my problem. I had been out of touch with myself.

We began to reminisce about our wedding trip, bicycling in the Adirondacks. It had been during World War II and not only had we virtually no money but travel restrictions and my short leave from the army had made us keep everything simple.

"We've made everything too complicated," I said, as if suddenly discovering a great wisdom. "Our home life . . . and my work . . ."

"It's so easy to avoid problems," my wife said quietly, "blocking them out with television, or leaning on the telephone as an easy answer. When we dig out I'm going home to see my father."

She went to the piano then and played, softly, making me realize that we had been getting our musical relaxation

canned for so long that I had forgotten how stimulating it could be fresh. I sat before the fire listening, watching the storm flex its great muscles out there in the night, thinking about what the snow was doing to us. It was bringing us much closer together.

We reached out, also, for books. That night, and the next morning (when we weren't talking) we finished novels that we had halfheartedly been pecking away at for months. Reading is fast vanishing from our world and we discovered anew the creative wonder of words, became aware again that the new world is living

When the storm abated—a tufted titmouse came in search of food.

an old lie, that, contrary to the old proverb, one picture is *not* always worth one thousand words.

When we awakened in the morning it was still snowing, but Nature is too much her own mistress to stay ominous. There was not a sound now, not a plane, just the wind, a blue jay battling it, brilliant blue feathers fluffed like a fur coat. The snow was now slowing into a mist, and an occasional clap of thunder would

come rolling to us from across the valley.

By noon that third day it stopped and the sun came out—and so did the wild ones. Made tame by hunger, the squirrels came shining from their tree dens as we shoveled hip-high snow from our back door and tossed them sunflower seeds. Juncos like little men in formal dress, dark bodies and light fronts, fox sparrows with tiger-striped breasts, the dainty silver, black-throated chickadees, the tufted titmice, the long-billed nuthatches, all coming close and twittering thanks as we gave them food. A flock of evening grosbeaks swept in as goldenly exotic as jungle birds. A shy cardinal sat in a birch tree, a blaze of fire in the snow, and we stood in amazement watching little heads poke up through the snow like fish breaking the surface of a pond. The chipmunks had shaken off their halfhearted hibernation and were surfacing, ballooning cheeks with sunflower seeds, then vanishing again.

The earth had been swept sparklingly clean by the white tide from the sky. Buildings were shingled in snow, tree limbs were swollen three times normal size. Stone fences were waves breaking in a white sea, wind had sculptured drifts into surrealistic art. White pine and spruce trees were sprayed in gay tinsel that shone with an electric light. The old scars and slashes of the earth were magically healed, snow flowed gracefully over ditches and fences, over stone piles and brush heaps in frozen ripples that glistened like white gold in the sun. Laurel bushes had come alive again in huge white blooms, the junipers had become a tiny replica of the alps, the honeysuckle hung in fragile lace from the house.

There came the scrape of the snowplow as it entered the drive. We were sorry to hear it. For three days we had lived in a pure white country that had set us free for a while. Snowfree.

Jack Denton Scott

Snow Fun

Creating colored icicles,
making frost pictures, capturing snowflakes
on velvet—these are a few
cold weather projects your family may want to
investigate this winter.

*I*f the windows in your house are not protected by storm glass, you may notice that on very cold days beautiful fairyland scenes will sometimes form on the inside panes. Frost occurs inside your house in the same way it occurs outside in the fields. Only in this case it is the warm water vapor in the indoor air that touches the pane, and is quickly chilled. Usually the frost crystals first develop around tiny bumps or specks of dust on the glass—and keep growing.

You can make a print of a frost picture on a bright, sunny morning before the rays heat the outside pane and melt the design. Try this experiment. You will need 8″ by 10″ sheets of blueprint paper and two shallow pans large enough to hold the paper spread out flat. Half fill each pan with clear water. To one of the pans add a tablespoonful of peroxide.

With cellophane tape, quickly fasten to the glass a sheet of blueprint paper with the sensitive side toward the pane. Press it against the frost design. The sunlight will turn parts of the paper pale blue. The frost pattern stays white on the paper. This takes about two minutes. Then spread the paper in the pan of plain water for a few minutes; next put it in the pan that has peroxide in it. When the blue is just the shade you want, spread the paper flat to dry. Collecting frost prints is an interesting hobby.

*T*ry working hand-in-hand with nature to create colorful icicles. If you would like to make these special rainbow treats, get an empty can and punch small holes in it: two holes along the top edges through which you put a string handle; and a very small hole in the bottom for water to drip through slowly enough to form icicles.

In another container mix a few drops of food coloring with some water. Mix as many colors as you have containers to hold the liquid. On a cold day, hang each can on a tree branch in your yard, and then pour the water into it. (Note: If the day is very cold, the water may freeze in the can before the icicles form. You may have to wrap something around the can to insulate it and keep the water from freezing.) Although it may take several different tries, the final result will be your own rainbow variety of homegrown icicles.

*W*hy not try to capture several snowflakes at once so that you can examine them closely? Staple a piece of black velvet onto a square of cardboard. Hold the cardboard under the falling snow, and in just a few seconds you will have a collection of snowflakes.

The black velvet background shows off each delicate snow crystal. Look closely with a magnifying glass. No two crystals are ever the same.

The Snow Maiden
СНЕГУРОЧКА

Once upon a time and long ago in Russia, there lived an old man named Ilya, and his wife, Fedota. They had everything they needed: a fine cottage, a cow, two sheep, and a very privileged cat who was allowed to sleep in the warmest spot in the house—the little shelf above the stove. But the old people weren't entirely happy. For alas, they had no children to gladden their declining years.

So it happened that one day during the coldest month of the winter, there was a great storm which blanketed the landscape with a glistening cover of fresh, white snow. With the snow's arrival all the children of this tiny village—behaving like children everywhere—abandoned their chores and studies to go outside and play. Merrily, they careened their way through the narrow streets on sleds, tried out a pair of homemade skis, threw snowballs—and they even built a snowman!

Sitting in his chair beside the warm stove, the old man watched the children as they frolicked happily outside his window. After a while, he turned to his wife saying, "Dear, why are we both inside on such a lovely winter's day? Although we are no longer young, we should be outside and building a fine snowman of our own."

As it turned out, the old woman was also in a playful mood that day. "All right, Ilya," she said. "We will go outside. But instead of a snowman, let's build a snowdaughter; and we will call her the little Snow Maiden."

No sooner had Fedota expressed her de-

40

sire than the old couple went out to their garden to build a snowdaughter. Two long hours they worked, carefully sculpturing their little child of snow. For eyes, they used beads of the brightest blue imaginable; and on her snow white cheeks they carved two little dimples. When they finished, the old man and the old woman couldn't take their eyes off the beautiful little Snow Maiden which they had created.

As they stared in disbelief, the tiny snow-child began to come to life. Blinking her lovely blue eyes, she smiled shyly at the old couple. And then she gracefully raised her arms to brush some loose snow from her forehead. As she stepped from her snowy birthplace, the little Snow Maiden moved to embrace her new parents. Placing an icy kiss on each of their cheeks she said, "Be not alarmed, your prayers have been answered."

Drawing a deep breath, Fedota turned to her husband and exclaimed, "We now have a living daughter—little Snow Maiden!"

Each day the old couple rejoiced anew in the child which had brought them both happiness and love. Not only was she gentle and kind, but she was also very clever. The village children flocked daily to the once lonely cottage to be entertained by the Snow Maiden's quick wit, and the merry little songs which she composed in her head at a moment's notice. At the sound of the children's voices ringing with laughter, the aging parents would pause in their chores to glance with pride upon their model daughter.

The little Snow Maiden grew very quickly—and each hour she became more beautiful. Ilya and Fedota never tired of looking at her. Her eyes were as blue as the sky above, and her lovely hair, which was bound in two, long, silken braids, hung far down her back. But alas, her lips and cheeks were pale—as pale as the white snow which falls from heaven.

As the days passed, and the winter slowly warmed into spring, the Snow Maiden became reluctant to venture from the cottage. More and more now she chose to remain in the cool shade provided by the thick walls and roof of her house. Inside, removed from her friends who chose to play outdoors, she would sadly think on the crisp winter days far beyond her reach—and of birds singing on snow-covered branches.

When spring moved towards summer, flowers began to bloom in the garden, and the grain ripened golden in the fields. Still the Snow Maiden sat sadly in the cool shadows of her room, seldom venturing outside. When she did so, she would carefully seek the shade of the tallest trees.

She was happiest now when the nights came and the temperature would drop. Asleep, she would dream that once again she was outside in winter's frosty landscape. But as soon as she would awake to see the sun climbing in the morning sky, she would break into tears.

The old couple grew worried about their daughter who had become so melancholy. Hugging her close, Fedota asked, "Are you well, dear?" But to this question the child

only responded, "Please be not troubled."

One fine day it happened that several of the Snow Maiden's friends decided to go into the woods to gather wild berries. As the children approached the cottage, they began to call to their old playmate to accompany them. "Come with us, Snow Maiden!"

At first, the little Snow Maiden was hesitant to leave the cool darkness of her room. However, the old couple, who felt that their daughter needed cheering up, said, "Dear child, go outside and have a good time with your friends." So not to disobey her parents, or appear rude to her playmates, the Snow Maiden picked up a basket for her berries and followed her friends.

But the distance was great, and the day was very warm. Feeling weak, the little Snow Maiden lagged farther and farther behind. "Hurry up," her playmates kept calling.

They were crossing a sunlit field which adjoined the woods when one of the youths stopped and began to play a merry little tune on his pipe. The Snow Maiden took this opportunity to lean wearily against a tree which provided some respite from the sun's heat.

Hearing the music, several of the village girls joined hands and began to dance in a circle. "Come join us," they cried gaily to the Snow Maiden. But there was no answer.

Turning from their game to the tree where the Snow Maiden had been resting, they saw no one. There was only a small mound of snow, and beside it was the basket which she had been carrying.

For days the villagers searched and searched for the little child of the snow. But she was never again seen.

As for Ilya and Fedota, the old couple, they never gave up hope that their child would come home to them. At the beginning of each new winter season they would console each other by saying, "Perhaps this year she will return."

Wildlife in Winter

The bitter wind unheeded blew,
From ripening corn the pigeons flew,
The partridge drummed i' the wood, the mink
Went fishing down the river-brink.
In fields with bean or clover gay,
The woodchuck, like a hermit gray,
   Peered from the doorway of his cell;
The muskrat plied the mason's trade,
And tier by tier his mud-walls laid;
And from the shagbark overhead
   The grizzled squirrel dropped his shell.

from *Snow-Bound* A Winter Idyl
—John Greenleaf Whittier

Peering from its sheltering tree hollow, this raccoon has just awakened from a torpid winter sleep. If the weather isn't pleasing, it will return to the den to nap a little longer. Several families may make their winter den together in the North; in the South, the raccoon stays active all year.

When North Winds Blow

For some wildlife a snowfall means new adventure, but for most it means additional challenges and dangers. Following a heavy snow, the playful river otter (below) prepares to career down a riverbank. Like a tobogganer it slides until hitting bottom, pauses to clean its fur, and then begins all over again.

While the otter frolics, a hungry red squirrel (opposite) ventures out on a frosty limb to nibble on the seeds of a spruce cone.

The Season's First Storm

*Five animals struggle to survive when
winter makes its appearance.
Taken by surprise, the ground-dwelling
meadowlark (left) is snowed in.*

The first snowfall of the winter began late in the afternoon. The big white flakes quickly covered the dry brown grasses and weeds in the field. The snow continued to fall through the night, making a deep layer. Its arrival affected the lives of all the creatures living in the field. For some the snow brought protection and made it possible for them to live through the winter. For others it meant hardship. It might even mean the end of life.

The meadow mouse

When the first flakes began to fall on the field the meadow mouse scurried to his nest in a big clump of dried grass. There he lay through the long winter night, sleeping fitfully as the snow built a white roof over the nest.

When morning came the mouse tried to poke his head out of the grass. Since he had been born only the past summer, he didn't know what snow was! His soft nose twitched to catch some smell that would tell him what the strange stuff was. When the warmth of his breath melted a tiny hole in the white wall, the mouse began to enlarge it by using his feet. Soon he was digging a tunnel with ease through the soft covering.

During the summer and fall the mouse had traveled about the field along pathways cut through the grass by the many mice living there. Now in winter the mouse would move through tunnels he dug in the snow. These would protect him from the cold and help to hide him from his enemies, the fox and the owl.

After tunneling for a short distance the mouse found the top of a buried weed. Several hard, fat seeds were still fastened to it. The meadow mouse was very hungry and began to eat. He was so busy eating, he didn't hear the sounds of digging overhead. Suddenly there was a shower of snow as the ceiling of the tunnel began to cave in. The mouse sensed danger and dashed down the tunnel. It seemed a good place to hide.

The chipmunk

In her burrow, several feet below the surface of the field, the chipmunk never knew that the snow had come. She had just awakened from her light sleep of hibernation and was stirring about in the dark chamber.

Since she had not put on extra weight as the woodchuck does before entering its burrow for the winter, she was hungry. The chipmunk pulled a stored acorn from under her bed of twigs and grasses and began to eat.

So far this winter the chipmunk had been lucky. The temperature of the earth around the burrow had not dropped below freezing. If it had, the chipmunk might have died. Now she would probably be safe. The new snow would act like a thick blanket to protect the ground and the creatures in it from the bitter cold above.

The chipmunk ate several more nuts before she curled up into a ball, tucked her head under her tail and went back to sleep. Her stomach was comfortably full now.

The meadowlark

The meadowlark was late in migrating to her winter home in a distant coastal marsh. Seeing the approaching snowstorm, she flew into the lower branches of an alder bush growing at the edge of the field. The bird fluffed up her bright yellow and black feathers, trapping the warmth of her body, and went to sleep. While she slept the snow piled up around the bush, but in the space under the branches, the bird stayed warm and dry.

When she awoke in the morning the meadowlark was in trouble! She could not fly out of the heavy, drifted, wet snow that covered the bush. Her struggles to free herself only brought a shower of loose snow tumbling in about her. By late afternoon the bird had managed to get her head above the snowdrift, but she was still trapped and too exhausted to try to free herself any further. She was the prisoner of the season's first storm.

The red fox

The red fox began his search for food almost as soon as the snow stopped falling. During the past week he had been feeding on berries and the remains of a rabbit, but the wind had covered that food with deep drifts of snow.

Several times during the morning he heard mice in their tunnels. But each time that he dug through the snow the mice had already gone!

It was now late in the afternoon and the fox

While the red fox (opposite) is poised in anticipation of a savory meal, the tiny chipmunk (above) settles down to a long winter's sleep with its cache of acorns.

hadn't eaten all day. Suddenly he saw the head of the meadowlark poking up through the snow. The fox sensed immediately that the bird was in trouble and could easily be captured. Just as the fox reached her the bird made a last desperate effort. The white crust broke and the meadowlark flew off awkwardly. The disappointed fox returned to his search as the sky darkened into dusk. He would have to find something else to ease his hunger.

A short while later he crossed the fresh tracks of the meadow mouse. The mouse had left the safety of his snow tunnel, not seeming to know the difference between the dim light in the tunnel and the evening dusk. The fox ran along the trail of footprints and almost caught up to the mouse as he disappeared into a snowbank. The fox dug frantically in the snow with his paws. Just as the fox uncovered him, the mouse tried to dash away, but this time he could not escape. The red fox was too quick.

The white-tailed deer

From her hiding place in the trees at the edge of the field the white-tailed deer looked out. It was early evening. The deer had been waiting, testing the air for smells and sounds that might mean danger. Just awhile ago she had seen a fox run by, then heard the faint squeal of a mouse. Now all was quiet!

The deer moved slowly into the field. It was hard for her to walk. Her sharp hoofs broke through the snow's crust and she sank down into the deep snow. In a low swampy part of the field the deer stopped to eat the twigs on a young tree. If it was a hard winter she would find no grasses, ferns or other low plants to feed on until the snows melted next spring. If there were too many other deer nearby, the twigs they could reach would be gone in a couple of months. Then the deer would face starvation.

Before she finished eating, a sound startled the deer. She bounded awkwardly across the field, her tail held high. Now and then she fell trying to avoid the deep drifts in her path. When she reached the dark shadows of the woods, the deer disappeared into the trees. As she did, a round white moon came out from behind the clouds, its light turning the first snowfall of winter into a sparkling field of diamonds.

Robert Dunne

White-tailed deer do not generally congregate in herds, although they may assemble in "yards" when deep snow makes it hard to find food. In harsh winters when rooting for nuts and grasses becomes difficult, the deer may browse on tree branches which the weight of the snow has bent within reach.

The Living Snow

When cold days arrive, the tiny song sparrow (top left) will fluff its feathers to trap layers of insulating warm air beneath.

Ruffed grouse, shown in an 1867 Currier and Ives print (center), can extend a fringe of scales from either side of each toe, enabling the grouse to stay atop deep snow.

Weighing only half as much as its cousin the jackrabbit, the varying hare (top right) can skim easily across the surface powder.

Trudging home in a snowstorm several years ago, flakes blowing, air snapping, I heard a bird sing softly in the wind. I was astonished, for the song was contented on this wild twilight. Plunging through a deep drift, I lifted a hemlock bough and saw a small sparrow on a brown twig. . . . The bird, puffed like a ball in the cup of frost, made comfortable chirping sounds, for he probably had not been so warm since winter began as on this first evening of snow.

As I gently replaced the bough I understood why the sparrow sang. To the bright-eyed bird, as to all life wintering in northern climates, the snow is as welcome as the rain and the sun. It is a comfort and a protection.

Most people, as they growl and dig with their snow shovels, forget that in the world of the birds and beasts and plants, snow is not a nuisance, but a vital ladder to food, a warm shelter, an insulator, a bridge, and material for animal cities.

I first became aware of the importance of snow as a ladder while my husband and I were visiting a friend and woodsman near Cobalt, Canada. Around his home were many leaping snowshoe rabbits, big white hares of the North that have developed wide furry feet to stay on top of the snow. The woodsman looked about his snowy yard and commented that the rabbits had almost eaten themselves out of food. Every twig they could reach by standing on their toes was snipped off with the slanted bite of their long teeth. I asked if there was danger of their starving. My friend squinted at the sky, sized up a typical snow cloud with its soft fuzzy edges and said that they would all be fine in the morning. "There'll be another rung on the big snow ladder," he commented.

"There's about a foot of snow in that cloud. It'll lift the rabbits to fresh twigs and stems."

Sometimes wildlife can't wait for the ladder to fall and they make their own. I was fascinated one winter day to see a grouse fashion a snow step. He was picking dried grapes off a vine in a nearby woods, and he ate until there were no more grapes in reach. He stretched to one above, could not quite get it, hopped for it and missed. Then, whether in frustration or knowledge, he scratched in the snow. The flakes piled into a mound, the bird stepped on it and snatched his prize.

The birds and beasts have developed some clever devices to keep on top of the snow. The grouse has little horny scutes, or discs, that spread out on either side of the toes and act as snow rafts. The ptarmigan grows feathers on his feet. The Canadian lynx has enormous paws—almost twice the size of those of his southern cousin, the bobcat. In addition these northern animals are lighter in weight so that there is not much pressure on their ingenious snowshoes. The naturalist, Ernest Thompson Seton, weighed the white hares of the North and found they were only half as heavy as the jackrabbits of Kansas.

But snowshoes can be troublesome for these birds and beasts when there is thawing and freezing and icing. . . . The birds pull their feet into their feathers to de-ice them, and the lynx sits down on his paws.

Most of the creatures that winter in the snow have been forced to make use of one of the outstanding physical properties of snow—its poor conductivity of heat. Mice and several species of birds, porcupines and shrews go down *under* the snow, where the white crystals hold their body heat like a mountain of insulation.

I have seen pheasants flutter their wings and wedge themselves into a snow pocket, and grouse fly headfirst into a snowbank for the night. More flakes are welcome, for they blanket the birds from the biting cold. The danger is crusting, and often birds are iced under the snow. If not thawed out by the sun within a day and a half they may never get out of their beds.

As an insulator for plants there is nothing better than snow. A snowless winter in Vermont virtually wiped out the young trees and bushes. And one year in my own town we all wondered why the forsythia bloomed only at the bottom two feet of every bush in town. Finally as we looked we recognized that the blossoms marked the snowline of the past winter. All the buds buried by a deep snow bloomed radiantly. Those above had been frozen to death by a week of unusual sub-zero weather.

Some seeds, it is now known, cannot germinate without the snow of winter. The peach seed needs a period of cold; not a deep freeze, but the gentle kind of chill a snowstorm brings to unfold its leaves and roots. Snow is also a water bank, holding the moisture of winter until spring gently releases it to the valleys and fields.

Meanwhile this treasure creates a new environment that must be coped with by nature. Deer and moose, cottontails and squirrels beat down trails for easier travel, as deliberately as you shovel your walk.

My uncle, on a hunting trip in the mountains of Pennsylvania, awakened in the night during a snowstorm to hear a herd of deer nearby tramping and snapping twigs and limbs as they kept their yard open. In the morning, when the last snowflake had settled, my uncle found their acre neatly packed, with grasses and mosses showing above the snow. Like wheel spokes other trails led out into the hills to pantries of grass they needed to keep alive.

Coyotes find hunting easier in snow. They are light enough to stay afloat in an ordinary snow. The deer and hoofed animals are not, and a coyote will chase a deer off his trail and bog him down in deep snow where he can take him easily.

Because nature does not let a good idea go to waste, other animals benefit from packed trails. When the deer bed down to sleep at dawn, the birds descend upon their open yards to pick up seeds and nuts kicked up by the sharp feet.

The most fascinating use that snow has been put to by the creatures of the wild is its development as cities. Under the snow, drilled, packed, dug, bitten, are millions of rooms and tunnels and roadways put there by the mice and shrews and marmots and moles, until a cross-section of a week-old snow would look like Swiss cheese.

The snow is appreciated by almost every animal that digs in the ground. Here is a medium just as warm, just as safe, as the earth, but one which can be tunnelled and carved with a nose or a hot breath. It is a glorious relief to the hard-digging beasts of the earth.

On the rock slopes of the west and the north, the pikas or conies—bright mountain rabbits with short ears and big eyes and no tails to get cold—live their daily lives under tons of snow, for they perforate the winter cover to live. Sitting rooms are propped with rocks, zig-zag halls lead under rocks where snowflakes never fall, corridors lead to "barns" of sweet grasses that the animals cut, dried and stored during the short summer months.

Life is so vigorous under the snow among the conies that occasionally word of their activity gets to the top side of the world. A famous western naturalist was traveling north with his dog team along an Alaskan River bank when he heard a cony squeak. He looked about him but saw only six feet of snow lying everywhere across the land. He listened, and the bleak white snow was busy with cony voices. Then he realized he was hearing the cony town under his feet. The little animals had heard him coming and were scolding him from six feet below.

Most wild animals, dogs and children love the snow. Minks and weasels play in it, leaping like darning needles in and out. They also travel through it, and perform their mad deeds of death under its cover.

One year my husband and I raised two minks to study. When the first snow came we turned these pets into the yard to observe them. We did not observe them long; they treated the snow like water, jack-knifed and dove under. There was not even a moving hump to mark their travels. Hastily we began to dig them out. Suddenly I leaped in pain. A mink was attached to my ankle above my boot, chittering as joyfully as if I were a mouse he had tracked down and captured.

Mice and shrews, weasels and otters, all carve roads and rooms beneath the snow. But the star-nosed mole makes cloverleaves and roller coasters, turnpikes and apartments, faster than anyone.

A friend of mine was mapping a mole's tunnel for a science journal. He came by the house one day to report that he could not dig with a shovel one half as fast as the mole digs with his nose and feet. The tired mammalogist declared the snow to be the mole's true medium. "He gets downright inspired," my friend commented, "when released from the confines of the earth to the freedom of the light crystals."

But on a winter's day when the air is clean and the sun bright, it is the top of the snow for me! For upon this white paper of winter are written, in talons and claws, hooves and noses, the most dramatic who-done-it stories I have ever read.

My favorite is the story of the missing pheasant, written in a farmyard in Ann Arbor, Michigan. I came down the farmer's lane early one morning to see that a pheasant had walked under the rail fence in the early dawn. He had found a bite to eat, a rose hip. He had picked out the seeds, scattered the pulp and walked on. Then something frightened him—his steps were far apart, running. Whatever it was vanished—his tracks closed again.

The pheasant was circling the field toward the woods when I saw that he was not long for this world. A fox track—one round hole behind the other in single file—fell in behind the pheasant's. I walked forward to read the sad ending; but it was not there. Suddenly the fox trail turned and walked away. The pheasant trail went on. Then down near the fence, I read in the torn snow the ending of the tale—slashes, struggle marks, footprints and feathers said the pheasant was dead, and gone. But the fox had not done it. I wondered who had. I looked closely at the marks in the snow, and made out the fuzzy X footprints and finger wing marks of the great horned owl of the forest! He had snatched the prize before the fox could strike, and winged away.

There are humorous stories in the snow, like the one written by a meadow mouse under my woodpile. On an icy day, in sleet and cold, he ran out a few steps, looked at the dreary world, and clearly said in three returning footsteps, "it ain't fit out for man nor beast."

And now it is winter again. I wait for the quiet snow to cover the fence and the hill so that I can go walking in the storm and feel the cold crystals on my cheeks and lips. As I trudge I will watch the bird fly to his pine tree and the rabbit bed down in his brush with a sense of comfort, I will know that the snow is as much a part of our world as the night, and like the night, the birds and beasts live gently with it.

Jean George

Gingerly treading a course along a fallen tree, a red fox left its tracks in the snow (above). In winter, the toe pads on the fox's feet are nearly concealed by heavy fur.

While hoofed animals—such as deer and antelope—bog down in deep drifts, the coyote (left) is light enough to stay afloat and overtake them.

Who's Been Walking in My Woods?

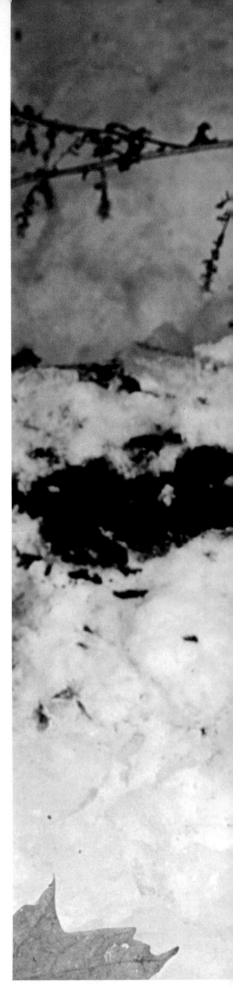

If you are a good detective, you can easily decipher some of the clues that wildlife leaves behind during the winter months. One way to study the habits of wild creatures is to follow their footprints, or tracks. From these markings you can often figure out whether the animal was walking, running, going to a definite destination, or just wandering.

Unique to each animal species are its tracks—although even experts may find it difficult to distinguish between them. If you look closely at the tracks of a cottontail rabbit (below), you will see the imprint of its two small forepaws set closely together, flanked by the two larger hind feet. Because all rabbits are primarily hoppers, hind feet often appear ahead of front feet when they leave tracks.

Snow trails sometimes tell stories, and some of them have abrupt endings. The prints of a tiny mouse may end in blood and fur, with the wing marks of a hawk or owl nearby.

Did you ever look closely at the chewed branches of shrubs and trees? The special toothmarks that animals leave can also identify them. A rabbit cleanly cuts a twig with its teeth, while a deer tears it. (See illustration on the left.) The deer's upper teeth are not good for cutting.

Stooping to observe where some fruits have fallen from a berry bush, you may notice that some mice have paid a visit. Their dizzy tracks go in and out over the snow and finally disappear down a little hole.

Seven familiar wild animals recently crossed this snowy field, leaving tracks behind them. Reading from left to right, the wildlife pictured are: opossum, cottontail rabbit, red fox, white-footed mouse, gray squirrel, raccoon, and long-tail weasel. Can you match the animals with their tracks? To find out how good a woodsman you are, turn the page upside down and check your answers.

A. Opossum; B. Weasel; C. Squirrel; D. Rabbit; E. Raccoon; F. Mouse—note wing marks made by the hawk that caught it; G. Fox.

Hiding and Abiding

Winter presents a special challenge for animals living in the wild. It is a time when the only bed around may be a white, fluffy one of snow; when freezing rains form ice on vegetation, and food supplies dwindle; when woodlands offer a cold retreat.

For many, however, the insulating qualities of snow can mean the difference between life and death. Buried beneath the forest duff, in burrows and rotting logs, dormant creatures depend on the cover of snow to prevent fatal temperature fluctuations.

For those who remain active during winter's worst, a thickened coat of fur or plumage retains the body heat. This air-trapping coat is another form of insulation.

A vegetarian, this moose cow (top) leads her calf in search of small plants which may lie buried underneath the crusty surface of the snow.

At Jackson Hole, a bull moose (right) may encounter drifts reaching up to its ears.

Each weighing under a pound at birth, the black bear cubs (left) were born to their mother as she slept in her cave. Although the bear hibernates in winter months, it can be easily awakened and will emerge from time to time as the weather improves.

63

The plight of the bison brought words of concern from Theodore Roosevelt: "The extermination of the buffalo has been a veritable tragedy of the animal world. . . . Its toughness and hardy endurance fitted it to contend with purely natural forces: to resist cold and the winter blasts, or the heat of a thirsty summer, to wander away to new pastures when the feed on the old was exhausted, to plunge over broken ground, and to plough its way through snow-drifts or quagmires. . . . But the seething myriads . . . vanished . . . before the inroads of the white hunters and the steady march of the oncoming settlers. Now they [the buffalo] are on the point of extinction."

Roosevelt closely observed the elk and noted while traveling through Yellowstone at the turn of the century, "As winter approaches . . . [the elk] divide, some going north and others south. The southern bands . . . winter out of the Park, for the most part in Jackson's Hole. . . . It was members of the Northern band [remaining in the Park] that I met. . . . In the winter, if they cannot get to open water, they eat snow; but in several places where . . . springs . . . are kept open all winter, we could see by the tracks that they had been regularly used by bands of elk."

The bison—or buffalo—no longer make long seasonal migrations southward as winter approaches. These largest of land mammals in North America are well adapted to cold weather. Thick layers of hide and hair protect them.

The wapiti or American elk (right) enjoys a sauna at one of Yellowstone's hot springs. Roosevelt thought that the proud carriage and lordly bearing of the elk made it one of the most majestic looking of all animals.

Theodore Roosevelt's
beloved buffalo and elk—
designed to cope with the elements

Over the eons of evolution, wildlife has developed many ways of adapting to its surroundings. One is camouflage—that protective coloring which allows an animal to blend in with its surroundings so that it is scarcely visible.

Camouflage can work as an offensive and a defensive technique. Some animals protect themselves by hiding from their enemies, while others use camouflage to launch surprise attacks on prey.

As winter approaches some animals shed their summer colors to adopt new coats of hiding white. For palefaces such as the polar bear and the mountain goat, their cream-colored fur is as permanent as their year-round snowy homes.

As the year progresses –
some animals change color
to match the landscape.

When cold weather comes to the tundra, the Arctic fox sheds its brown fur while growing a thick coat of winter white (left). This new disguise helps conceal the fox as it hunts lemmings on the snow.

Sporting a fresh growth of creamy fur, the least weasel (far left) takes on a protective coloration which will serve it well both as the hunter and the hunted.

An early snow caught this varying hare, or snowshoe rabbit (above), still wearing its summer-brown ears and legs.

Although the hair of the gray or timber wolf (left) does not change in color, individuals may vary in appearance, from pepper-gray to almost white, depending on how far north they live.

The Legend of the Mountain Goat

Long ago some tribes moved into the Mountain Goat country and settled there. And the men . . . were as wild and savage as their country. They raided other villages, . . . burned and looted them, and carried home captives, (including the) young son of a chief.

Captured-Man was deeply troubled by the ways of the mountain people. . . . He knew that animals should be killed only for food or clothing, and the scraps should always be burned. But his masters killed all the mountain goats they could, and left the carcasses lying where they fell. They carried off only the horns for spoons, and a little of the choicest meat. . . .

"If we take what we need and burn the scraps, the animal's spirit will recover," Captured-Man told them.

But they refused to listen.

One fall they took a baby goat from its mother, and carried it home as a plaything for the children.

Only severe storms can force this mountain goat kid from its home in the jagged peaks around Alaska's Riggs Glacier (left).

And the children, having no more sense than the parents, held it and fondled it and snatched it back and forth, and never let the poor thing rest. The older people heard the children's noise, but they shrugged it off, saying, "It's only that baby goat."

Then Captured-Man shoved the children aside and took the little goat away. "Beware!" he told them. "The Mountain Goat Chief is watching over his people!"

But the children laughed.

Captured-Man kept the little goat overnight, and fed it, and let it rest on his blanket in the corner. In the morning he painted a scratch on its face with his own red face paint, and carried it far away from the village before he turned it loose. The little goat nuzzled his hand for a moment and bounded off.

The year passed, and the people of the village forgot all about the children and the baby goat. Then, when the moon was low and fat, messengers came to invite the hunters to a feast. The strangers were wrapped in long gray blankets, and they left when their message was delivered and refused to have anything to eat. But the mountain people were fond of a feast, and they went into their houses and dressed themselves in their ceremonial garments. They wore headdresses hung with the tails of bears, and one had an earring of abalone and one had a mantle embroidered with puffin beaks.

While the fathers were getting ready for the feast, the children followed the strangers out of town. What was their amazement, then, to see the tall, grim men throw off their blankets and go bounding up the canyon! The children ran home, their eyes popping out with the wonder of what they had seen.

"They've thrown off their blankets and turned into Goats!" they shouted. And the mothers cuffed them and told them to tell the truth.

Preferring to live near the snowfields above timberline, the surefooted mountain goat finds its hooves—with their sharp rims and soft inner pads—perfect for climbing over rocks and ice.

71

The men set out, taking Captured-Man with them in case he should be useful. Soon, following the trail that the messengers had pointed out, they came in sight of a great square house with white smoke billowing from the smoke hole. Behind it rose a dark cliff, and it looked as if the house were part of the mountain.

As they drew near, the door opened, and out filed the people wearing long gray blankets and the headdress of the Mountain Goat. Singing and dancing to welcome the strangers to the feast, they made a circle around the hunters and swept them into the house.

They were seated all together at the front. But one young man wearing red face paint singled out Captured-Man and led him aside. He made him sit in the central space, with his back against a heavy house post. And all through the serving of the four courses, he watched to see that he had the choicest food. Captured-Man was astonished at this, for he was used to scraps. His masters watched him angrily, but there was nothing they could do.

Then the ceremony started. After singing the songs of the four guardian spirits of the house, they heard the eerie whistling of the winter wind. Then up through the center of the earthen floor came a slender white peak like the icy top of a mountain. It rose until its top went out through the smoke hole, and wide cracks opened in the floor, and the earth shuddered.

While the hunters stared speechless at the mountain in the house, the rattles began to shake. A one-horned Goat appeared upon the mountain, and lightly it leaped from crag to crag down to the level of the people. Then it sailed through the air, just clearing their heads, and struck the front of the house with its cloven hoof.

With a noise like thunder, the house gave way. The whole front wall went sliding down, and the boards were wrenched loose, and the roof pitched downward . . . into clouds of smoking rubble.

When silence came at last and the dust had cleared away, Captured-Man found himself outdoors, on the open side of the mountain. The house post behind him had changed to stone, and a dizzy chasm lay at his feet, with the blue sea beating on wicked rocks below. He was pressed against the cliff on a narrow ledge that faded away to nothing on his right. To the left it climbed steeply around the shoulder of the mountain.

But now, as he watched, there came leaping down it a young Goat.

"Have no fear, my friend," said the Mountain Goat. "You rescued me from the children once, so when the Goat Chief killed the wicked hunters, you were saved from the landslide."

Captured-Man shrank from the rocky chasm and covered his eyes.

"How am I to ever get off this terrible mountain?" he asked.

"I'll lend you my shoes," said the Mountain Goat. "Now watch what I do, and say what you hear me say."

Then, with a "Goat foot leap!" and "Goat foot jump!" and matching the rhythm of the magic words, the Mountain Goat skipped lightly down the face of the treacherous cliff. He circled back up and let Captured-Man put on his goatskin and his cloven shoes. Trusting in the power of the Mountain Goat's magic, he said, "Goat foot leap!" and his left foot held, and "Goat foot jump!" and his right foot held. Then, "Over the chasm, over the glacier! Leap! Jump! Leap!" And away he went, with the clear sky above him and the wild wind singing in his ears. He leaped down the mountain, free as a goat, free of his masters at last.

Leaving the goatskin and cloven shoes, Captured-Man returned to the village and called the children together. He led them back to the high places and made them gather up the bleached bones of the goats and burn them.

These boys were better hunters than their fathers, for they followed Captured-Man's advice, never killing without reason, and treating the bones with respect. Captured-Man became Head-Man among them, and the Mountain Goat was the crest of his family for all generations.

Indian totem poles
feature symbolic animal carvings

For the Tlingit, Haida, Tsimshian, and Kwakiutl tribes of America's Pacific Northwest, winter was a time to tell stories of wildlife, among them *The Legend of the Mountain Goat. Nuyemsida Melxtlu*, it is called in Kwakiutl.

Winter months were the time, too, when the tribes would carve elaborate totem poles. The original purpose of these poles was to provide support for the roofs of their houses. Just as the hero "Captured Man" was given the mountain goat as his personal totem, so each family collected its own guardian animal spirits which they carved and painted on these unique poles. The richer and more powerful families would display so many symbolic crests that their totems reached heights of up to 80 feet.

For the sacred animals there were special symbols that were instantly recognized. For example, the raven was always carved with a long, straight beak (as in the Tlingit totem at left). The slit in the lower lip of Fog Woman, goddess of salmon (below), distinguishes her from a man.

In time, the pole with its column of sacred animal designs became the trademark of the Northwest Coastal Indians.

Reindeer and Caribou and the Spirit of Christmas

Reindeer (left), the miraculous animals of the far north that carry Santa across the sky on a single enchanted night in December each year, have been celebrated in America in song, story, and poem for more than a hundred years. In the same magic circle live their close cousins, the wondrous caribou (above), of Alaska.

The Coming of St. Nicholas to America

According to legend, St. Nicholas arrived in America on the prow of the *Goede Vrouw*, which was carrying a group of Dutch folk eager to venture into the New World. This good bishop of Myra, whose carved likeness decorated the ship, had been revered in Holland for centuries for his generosity toward the poor. His new mission on this occasion was to watch over the valiant Hollanders who had dared to cross the ocean.

The *Goede Vrouw* landed at Communipaw, an Indian village on the New Jersey shore. Here the settlers began to build their homes, but when British eyes fell on the land, the Dutch decided to move on. And so Oloffe Van Kortlandt led a small group of his countrymen on a voyage of discovery—through New York Bay. Shipwrecked by the turbulent waters of Hell-gate, Van Kortlandt and his followers sought refuge on the island of Manna-hatta, to eat and rest and sleep.

"And the sage Oloffe," says Washington Irving, "dreamed a dream—and lo, the good St. Nicholas came riding over the tops of the trees, in that self-same wagon wherein he brings his yearly presents to children, and he descended hard by where the heroes of Communipaw had made their late repast. And he lit his pipe by the fire, and sat himself down and smoked; and as he smoked, the smoke from his pipe ascended into the air and spread like a cloud overhead. And Oloffe bethought him, and he hastened and climbed up to the top of one of the tallest trees, and saw that the smoke spread over a great extent of country; and as he considered it more attentively, he fancied that the great volume of smoke assumed a variety of marvellous forms, where in dim obscurity he saw shadowed out palaces and domes and lofty spires, all of which lasted but a moment, and then faded away. . . . And when St. Nicholas had smoked his pipe, he twisted it in his hatband, and laying his finger beside his nose, gave the astonished Van Kortlandt a very significant look; then, mounting his wagon, he returned over the treetops and disappeared. . . .

"And Van Kortlandt awoke from his sleep greatly instructed; and he aroused his companions and related his

dream, and interpreted it, that it was the will of St. Nicholas that they should settle down and build the city here . . ." on the new land.

The Dutch struck a good bargain with the Indians and bought the island of Manhattan, and promptly began building a fort. "Thus," says Irving, "having quietly settled themselves down, and provided for their own comfort, they bethought themselves of testifying their gratitude to the great and good St. Nicholas, for his protecting care, in guiding them to this delectable abode. To this end they built a fair and goodly chapel within the fort, which they consecrated to his name; whereupon he immediately took the town of New Amsterdam under his peculiar patronage, and he has ever since been, and I devoutly hope, will ever be, the tutelar saint of this excellent city.

"At this early period was instituted that pious ceremony, still religiously observed in all our ancient families of the right breed, of hanging up a stocking in the chimney on St. Nicholas eve; which stocking is always found

Two hundred and fifty years after the Dutch landed on Jersey's shore near Communipaw, their descendants could enjoy the view in Currier's "City of New York from Jersey City."

in the morning miraculously filled; for the good St. Nicholas has ever been a great giver of gifts, particularly to children.

. . . "Thus benignly fostered by the good St. Nicholas, the infant city thrived apace."

Stockings are hung, says an old legend, because once, long ago, the good St. Nicholas tossed a bag of gold for a young woman to use as her dowry, and it fell, by chance, into a stocking hung by the chimney to dry.

The Dutch in America celebrated St. Nicholas' day on December 6th, the date of his death, as had been their custom in Holland. And when the English took over the Dutch City of New Amsterdam and renamed it New York, they too hung stockings by the chimney, but on the eve of December 25th—the traditional date for the English celebration of Christmas.

The Night Before Christmas

Originally written for his children,
C.C. Moore's poem was illustrated by Thomas Nast,
whose drawing is complete with mice not
stirring but sound asleep.

'Twas the night before Christmas, when all through
　　the house
Not a creature was stirring, not even a mouse;
The stockings were hung by the chimney with care,
In hopes that St. Nicholas soon would be there;
The children were nestled all snug in their beds;
While visions of sugar-plums danced in their heads;
And mamma in her 'kerchief, and I in my cap,
Had just settled our brains for a long winter's nap;
When out on the lawn there arose such a clatter,
I sprang from the bed to see what what was the matter.
Away to the window I flew like a flash,
Tore open the shutters and threw up the sash.
The moon, on the breast of the new-fallen snow,
Gave the lustre of mid-day to objects below,
When, what to my wondering eyes should appear,
But a miniature sleigh, and eight tiny rein-deer,
With a little old driver, so lively and quick,
I knew in a moment it must be St. Nick.
More rapid than eagles his coursers they came,
And he whistled, and shouted, and called them by name;
"Now, Dasher! now, Dancer! now, Prancer and Vixen!
On, Comet! on, Cupid! on, Donder and Blitzen!
To the top of the porch! to the top of the wall!
Now dash away! dash away! dash away all!"
As dry leaves that before the wild hurricane fly,
When they meet with an obstacle, mount to the sky;
So up to the house-top the coursers they flew,
With the sleigh full of Toys, and St. Nicholas too.
And then, in a twinkling, I heard on the roof

The prancing and pawing of each little hoof —
As I drew in my head, and was turning around,
Down the chimney St. Nicholas came with a bound.
He was dressed all in fur, from his head to his foot,
And his clothes were all tarnished with ashes and soot;
A bundle of Toys he had flung on his back,
And he look'd like a pedlar just opening his pack.
His eyes — how they twinkled! his dimples how merry!
His cheeks were like roses, his nose like a cherry!
His droll little mouth was drawn up like a bow,
And the beard of his chin was as white as the snow;
The stump of a pipe he held tight in his teeth,
And the smoke it encircled his head like a wreath;
He had a broad face and a little round belly
That shook, when he laughed, like a bowl full of jelly.
He was chubby and plump, a right jolly old elf,
And I laughed, when I saw him, in spite of myself;
A wink of his eye and a twist of his head,
Soon gave me to know I had nothing to dread;
He spoke not a word, but went straight to his work,
And fill'd all the stockings; then turned with a jerk,
And laying his finger aside of his nose,
And giving a nod, up the chimney he rose;
He sprang to his sleigh, to his team gave a whistle,
And away they all flew like the down of a thistle.
But I heard him exclaim, ere he drove out of sight,
"Happy Christmas to all, and to all a good night."

Clement C. Moore,
1862, March 13th originally written
many years ago.

Some Creatures Were Stirring...

*In one of the best-loved
passages of Kenneth Grahame's* Wind
in the Willows, *field mice
arrive at Mole End and are invited
to stay for dinner.*

*Illustrated by
Ernest H. Shepard*

At Mole End, Rat and Mole were just preparing to settle down to dinner when sounds were heard from the fore-court without—sounds like the scuffling of small feet in the gravel and a confused murmur of tiny voices, while broken sentences reached them— 'Now, all in a line—hold the lantern up a bit, Tommy—clear your throats first—no coughing after I say one, two, three.—Where's young Bill?—Here, come on, do, we're all a-waiting——'

'What's up?' inquired the Rat, pausing in his labours.

'I think it must be the field-mice,' replied the Mole, with a touch of pride in his manner. 'They go round carol-singing regularly at this time of the year. They're quite an institution in these parts. And they never pass me over—they come to Mole End last of all; and I used to give them hot drinks, and supper too sometimes, when I could afford it. It will be like old times to hear them again.'

'Let's have a look at them!' cried the Rat, jumping up and running to the door.

It was a pretty sight, and a seasonable one, that met their eyes when they flung the door open. In the fore-court, lit by the dim rays of a horn lantern, some eight or ten little field-mice stood in a semicircle, red worsted comforters round their throats, their fore-paws thrust deep into their pockets, their feet jigging for warmth. With bright beady eyes they glanced shyly at each other, sniggering a little, sniffing and applying coat-sleeves a good deal. As the door opened, one of the elder ones that carried the lantern was just saying, 'Now then, one, two, three!' and forthwith their shrill little voices uprose on the air, singing one of the old-time carols that their fore-fathers composed in fields that were fallow and held by frost, or when snow-bound in chimney corners, and handed down to be sung in the miry street to lamp-lit windows at Yule-time.

> Villagers all, this frosty tide,
> Let your doors swing open wide,
> Though wind may follow, and snow beside,
> Yet draw us in by your fire to bide;
>   Joy shall be yours in the morning!
>
> Here we stand in the cold and the sleet,
> Blowing fingers and stamping feet,
> Come from far away you to greet—
> You by the fire and we in the street—
>   Bidding you joy in the morning!

> For ere one half of the night was gone,
> Sudden a star has led us on,
> Raining bliss and benison—
> Bliss to-morrow and more anon,
>   Joy for every morning!
>
> Goodman Joseph toiled through the snow—
> Saw the star o'er a stable low;
> Mary she might not further go—
> Welcome thatch, and litter below!
>   Joy was hers in the morning!

> And then they heard the angels tell
> 'Who were the first to cry Nowell?
> Animals all, as it befell,
> In the stable where they did dwell!
>   Joy shall be theirs in the morning!'

"The Year Santa Came Late"

This is a tale of the bleak, bitter Northland, where the frost is eternal and the snows never melt, where the wide white plains stretch for miles and miles . . . and where the Heavens at night are made terribly beautiful by the trembling flashes of the northern lights, and the green icebergs float in stately grandeur down the dark currents of the hungry polar sea. . . . The only cheerful thing about all this country is that far up within the Arctic Circle, just on the edge of the boundless snow plains, there is a big house . . . where lights shine all year round from the windows, and the wide halls are warmed by blazing fires. For this is the house of his beloved Saintship, Nicholas, whom the children the world over call Santa Claus.

Now every child knows this house is beautiful, and beautiful it is, for it is one of the most home-like places in the world. Just inside the front door is the big hall, where every evening after his work is done Santa Claus sits by the roaring fire and chats with his wife, Mamma Santa, and the White Bear. Then there is the dining room, and the room where Papa and Mamma Santa sleep, and to the rear are the workshops, where all the wonderful toys are made, and last of all the White Bear's sleeping room, for the White Bear has to sleep in a bed of clean white snow every night, and so his room is away from the heated part of the house.

But most boys and girls do not know much about the White Bear, for though he is really a very important personage, he has been strangely neglected by the biographers of Santa Claus. . . . He is not at all like the bears who carry off naughty children, and does not even belong to the same family as the bears who ate up the forty children who mocked at the Prophet's bald head. On the contrary, this bear is a most gentle and kindly fellow, and fonder of boys and girls than any one else in the world, except Santa Claus himself. He has lived with Papa Santa from time immemorial, helping him in his workshop, painting rocking horses, and stretching drum heads, and gluing yellow wigs on doll babies. But his principal duty is to care for the reindeer, those swift, strong, nervous little beasts, without whom the hobby horses and dolls and red drums would never reach the little children in the world.

One evening, on the twenty-third of December—the rest of the date does not matter—Papa Santa sat by the fire in the great hall, blowing the smoke from his nostrils, until his ruddy round face shone through it like a full moon through the mist. He was in a happier mood even than usual, for his long year's work in his shop was done, the last nail had been driven, the last coat of paint had dried. All the vast array of toys stood ready to go into the sealskin

bags and be piled into the sleigh for the children of the world.

Opposite him sat Mamma Santa, putting the last dainty stitches on a doll dress for a little sick girl somewhere down in the world. Mamma Santa never kept track of where the different children lived; Papa Santa and the White Bear attended to the address book. It was enough for her to know that they were children and good children, she didn't care to know any more. By her chair sat the White Bear, eating his dog sausage. The White Bear was always hungry between meals, and Mamma Santa always kept a plate of his favorite sausage ready for him in the pantry, which, as there was no fire there, was a refrigerator as well.

As Papa Santa bent to light his pipe once again, he spoke to the White Bear:

"The reindeer are all in good shape, are they? You've seen them tonight? There are no problems?"

"I gave them their feed and rubbed them down an hour ago, and I never saw them friskier. They ought to skim like birds tomorrow night. As I came away, though, I thought I saw the Were-Wolf Dog hanging around, so I locked up the stable."

"That was right," said Papa Santa,

With the icy glow of the Aurora Borealis in the night skies behind it, this cabin radiates the coziness of Santa's legendary home at the North Pole.

82

approvingly. "He was there for no good, depend on that. Last year he tampered with the harness and cut it so that four traces broke before I reached Norway."

Mamma Santa sent her needle through the fine cambric she was stitching with an indignant thrust, and spoke so emphatically that the little white curls under her cap bobbed about her face. "I cannot understand the perverse wickedness of that animal, nor what he has against you, that he should be forever troubling you, or against those World-Children, poor little innocents, that he should be forever trying to defraud them of their Christmas presents. He is certainly the meanest animal from here to the Pole."

"That he is," said Papa Santa, "and there is no reason for it at all. But he hates everything that is not mean as himself."

"I am sure, Papa, that he will never be at rest until he has brought about some serious accident. Hadn't the Bear better look about the stables again?"

"I'll sleep there tonight and watch, if you say so," said the White Bear, rapping the floor with his shaggy tail.

"O, there is no need of that, we must all get our sleep tonight, for we have hard work and a long journey before us tomorrow. I can trust the reindeer pretty well to look after themselves. Come, Mamma, come, we must get to bed." Papa Santa shook the ashes out of his pipe and blew out the lights, and the White Bear went to stretch himself in his clean white snow.

When all was quiet about the house, there stole from out the shadow of the wall a great dog, shaggy and monstrous to look upon. His hair was red, and his eyes were bright,

The Were-Wolf Dog of Willa Cather's story was a villain, but real-life wolves are intelligent, faithful, and social creatures. For the timber—or gray—wolf (left), this kind of threatening snarl is just a sign of defense.

like ominous fires. . . . and there was always a little foam about his lips as though he were raging with some inward fury. He carried his tail between his legs, for he was as cowardly as he was vicious. This was the wicked Were-Wolf Dog who hated everything; the beasts and the birds and Santa Claus and the White Bear, and most of all the little children of the world. Nothing made him so angry as to think that there really are good children in the world, little children who love each other, and are simple and gentle and fond of everything that lives, whether it breathes or blooms. For years he had been trying in one way and another to delay Santa Claus' journey so that the children would get no beautiful gifts from him at Christmastime . For the Were-Wolf Dog hated Christmas too, incomprehensible as that may seem. He was thoroughly wicked and evil, and Christmas time is the birthday of Goodness, and every year on Christmas Eve the rage in his dark heart burned anew.

He stole softly to the window of the stable, and peered in where the swift, tiny reindeer stood each in his warm little stall, pawing the ground impatiently. For on glorious moonlight nights like that the reindeer never slept, they were always so homesick for their freedom and their wide white snow plains.

"Little reindeer," called the Were-Wolf Dog, softly, and all the little reindeer pricked up their ears. "Little reindeer, it is a lovely night," and all the little reindeer sighed softly. They knew, ah, how well they knew!

"Little reindeer, the moon is shining as brightly as the sun does in the summer; the North wind is blowing fresh and cold, driving the little clouds across the sky like white sea birds. The snow is just hard enough to bear without breaking, and your brothers are running like wild things over its white crust. And the stars, ah, the stars, little brothers, they gleam like a million jewels, and glitter like icicles all over the face of the sky. Come, see how they sparkle."

The reindeer stamped impatiently in their little stalls. It was very hard. They wanted to be out racing freely with all the other reindeer.

"Come, little reindeer, let me tell you why all your brothers run toward the Polar Sea tonight. It is because tonight the northern lights will flash as they never did before, and the great streaks of red and purple and violet will shoot across the sky until all the people of the world shall see them, who never saw before. Listen, little reindeer, it is just the night for a run, a long free run, with no traces to tangle your feet and no sleigh to drag. Come, let us go, you will be back again by dawn and no one will ever know."

Dunder stamped in his stall, it made him long to be gone, to hear what the Were-Wolf Dog said. "No, no, we cannot, for tomorrow we must start with the toys for the little children of the world."

"But you will be back tomorrow. Just when the dim light is touching the tops of the icebergs and making the fresh snow red, you will be speeding home. Ah, it will be a glorious run, and you will see the lights as they never shone before. Do you not pant to feel the wind about you, little reindeer?"

Then Cupid and Blitzen could withstand his enticing words no longer, and begged, "Come, Dunder, let us go tonight. It has been so long since we have seen the lights, and we will be back tomorrow."

Now the reindeer knew well enough they ought not to go, but reindeer are not like people, and sometimes the things they want most awfully to do are the very things that they ought not to do. The thought of the fresh winds and their dear lights of the North and the moonlit snow drove them wild, for the reindeer love their freedom more than any other animal, and swift motion, and the free winds.

So the dog pried open the door, with the help of the reindeer forcing

it from within, and they all dashed out into the clear moonlight and scurried away toward the North like gleeful rabbits. "We will be back by morning," said Cupid. "We will be back," said Dunder. And, poor little reindeer, they loved the snow so well that it scarcely seemed wrong to go.

O, how fine it was to feel that wind in their fur again! They tossed their antlers in the fresh wind, and their tiny hoofs rang on the hard snow as they ran. They ran for miles and miles without growing tired, or losing their first pleasure in it. . . .

"Slower, slower, little reindeer, for I must lead the way. You will not find the place where the beasts are assembled," called the Were-Wolf Dog.

The little reindeer could no more go slowly than a boy can when the fire engines dash by. So they got the Were-Wolf Dog in the center of the pack and fairly bore him on with them. On they ran over those vast plains of snow that sparkled as brightly as the sky did above, and Dasher and Prancer bellowed aloud with glee. At last there lay before them the boundless stretch of the Polar Sea. Dark and silent it was, as mysterious as the strange secret of the Pole which it guards forever. Here and there where the ice floes had parted showed a crevice of black water, and the great walls of ice glittered like flame when the northern lights flung their red banners across the sky, and tipped the icebergs with fire. There the reindeer paused a moment for very joy, and the Were-Wolf Dog fell behind silently.

"Is the ice safe, old dog?" asked Vixen, calling to the Were-Wolf Dog.

"To the right it is, off and away, little reindeer. It is growing late," said the Were-Wolf Dog, shouting hoarsely; "To the right."

And the heedless little reindeer dashed on, never noticing that the wicked Were-Wolf Dog stayed behind on the shore. Now when they were out a good way upon the sea they heard a frightful cracking, grinding sound, such as the ice makes when it breaks up.

"To the shore, little brothers, to the shore!" cried Dunder, but it was too late. The wicked Were-Wolf Dog where he stood on the land saw the treacherous ice break and part, and the head of every little reindeer go down under the black water. Then he turned and fled over the snow, with his tail tighter between his legs than ever, for he was too cowardly to look upon his own evil work.

As for the reindeer, the black current caught them and whirled them down under the ice, all but Dunder and Dasher and Prancer, who at last rose to the surface and lifted their heads above the water.

"Swim, little brothers, we may yet make the shore," cried Dunder. So

among the cakes of broken ice that cut them at every stroke, the three brave little beasts began to struggle toward the shore that seemed so far away. A great chunk of ice struck Prancer in the breast, and he groaned and sank. Then Dasher began to breathe heavily and fell behind, and when Dunder stayed to help him he said, "No, no, little brother, I cannot make it. You must not try to help me, or we will both go down. Go tell it all to the White Bear. Goodbye, little brother, we will skim the white snow fields no more together." And with that he, too, sank down into the black water, and Dunder struggled on all alone.

When at last he dragged himself

In large herds, reindeer numbering in the thousands still assemble during post-calving and fall migration. The fawns shown above will lighten in color as they mature.

wearily upon the shore he was exhausted and cruelly cut and bleeding. But there was no time to be lost. Spent and suffering as he was, he set out across the plains.

Late in the night the White Bear heard someone tapping, tapping against his window and saw poor Dunder standing there all covered with ice and blood.

"Come out, brother," he gasped, "the others are all dead and drowned, only I am left. . . ."

hen the White Bear hastened out . . . and Dunder told him all about the cruel treachery of the Were-Wolf Dog.

"Alas," cried the White Bear, "and who shall tell Santa of this, and who will drag his sleigh tomorrow to carry the gifts to the little children of the world? Empty will their stockings hang on Christmas morning, and Santa's heart will be broken."

Then poor Dunder sank down in the snow and wept.

"Do not despair, Dunder. We must go tonight to the ice hummock where the beasts meet to begin their Christmas revels. Can you run a little longer, poor reindeer?"

"I will run until I die," said Dunder, bravely. "Get on my back and we will go." . . . And they sped away to the great ice hummock where the animals of the North all gather to keep their Christmas.

The ice hummock is a great pile of ice and snow right under the North Star, and all the animals were there drinking punches and wishing each other a Merry Christmas. There were seals, and fur otters, and white ermines, and whales, and bears, and many strange birds, and the tawny Lapland dogs that are as strong as horses. But the Were-Wolf Dog was not there. The White Bear paid no heed to any of them, but climbed up to the very top of the huge ice hummock. Then he stood up and cried out:

"Animals of the North, listen to me!" and all the animals ceased from their merrymaking and looked up to the ice hummock where the White Bear stood, looking very strange up there, all alone in the starlight.

"Listen to me," thundered the White Bear, "and I will tell you such a tale of wickedness and treachery as never came up among us before. This night the wicked Were-Wolf Dog . . . came to the reindeer of Santa Claus and with enticing words lured them

A nomad in the vast Arctic reaches, the giant polar bear can outrun even a reindeer over short distances.

northward, promising to show them the great lights as they never shone before. But black Death he showed them, and the bottom of the Polar Sea." Then he showed them poor bleeding Dunder, and told how all the tiny reindeer had been drowned and all the treachery of the Were-Wolf Dog. . . .

"Now, O animals," the White Bear went on, "who among you will go back with me and draw the sleigh full of presents down to the little World-Children, for a shame would it be to all of us if they should awaken and find themselves forgotten and their stockings empty."

But none of the animals replied . . .

"What," cried the White Bear. "Is there not one of you who will . . . take the place of our brothers who are now dead? . . ."

But the animals all thought of the wide plains and the stinging North wind and their scampers of old, and hung their heads and were silent. Poor Dunder groaned aloud, and even the White Bear had begun to despair, when there spoke up a poor old seal with but one fin, for he had fallen into the seal fishers' hands and been maimed. . . . "I am only an old seal who has been twice wounded by the hunters, and am a cripple, but lo, I myself will go with the White Bear, and though I can travel but a mile a day at best, yet will I hobble on my tail and my one fin until I have dragged the sleigh full of presents to the World-Children."

Then the animals were all ashamed of themselves, and the reindeer all sprang forward and cried, "We will go, take us!"

So the next day, a little later than usual, Santa Claus wrapped himself in his fur lap robes, and seven new reindeer, headed by Dunder, flew like the winged wind toward the coast of Norway. And if any of you remember getting your presents a little late that year, it was because the new reindeer were not used to their work yet, though they tried hard enough.

Willa Cather

89

Favorites of the Far North

Santa Claus couldn't have chosen a better team for his sleigh than the reindeer. Of course he had to use his own magic to make them trot on air, but otherwise reindeer are perfect for a journey that starts at the North Pole.

The reindeer was first domesticated in Siberia. Even today in Lapland and parts of Siberia, reindeer herds provide meat, milk, and hides. They are also used to pull heavy sleds.

The map on page 92 shows how wild reindeer came to North America many thousands of years ago. The slight differences in appearance between caribou and reindeer can be attributed to domestication, since they both belong to the same species.

Caribou is derived from an Indian word meaning "shoveler." It comes from the animal's habit of pawing the snow to find its main food: lichens and sedges. The caribou's "shovel" feet are a big help in wet, boggy areas like the Arctic tundra in summertime. The hooves spread apart, making the foot wider than it is long. The dewclaws—the two toes at the back of each foot—reach the ground and give extra support. In summer the hoof has a soft, spongy pad at its center. This dries up in winter and is covered with short hair which provides extra warmth. The outer edge of the hoof becomes hard which helps keep the animal from slipping on icy ground.

Caribou prefer to travel in herds, which may provide some measure of safety. They walk—marching to a strange, clicking beat caused by their tendons rubbing tightly against their heel bones. When alarmed, caribou can trot at better than 30 miles an hour. They carry their antler-crowned heads proudly and each leg is picked up high as though it had springs. They almost seem to be trotting on air—like Santa's reindeer.

The caribou's handsome, white-trimmed, gray-brown winter coat is made of hollow, air-filled hairs that insulate against Arctic cold. This hair also acts as a built-in life jacket and keeps the caribou floating high on the water when crossing rivers. Even the caribou's nose is covered with hair in winter. Their "shovel" feet make excellent paddles for swimming.

The caribou's main predator is the wolf. But a wolf cannot catch a healthy caribou. Wolves chase the herd until the old, the sick, and the weakest of the young drop out.

Today in North America there are four main subspecies of caribou:

Grant's caribou occupy much of Alaska from Unimak Island and the Alaska Peninsula to the Arctic Ocean.

Peary's caribou live in northern Greenland, on Ellsmere and neighboring Arctic islands. They, like the

Unlike the reindeer which may have been domesticated as early as 12,000 B.C., caribou (left) have proven stubborn about entering into man's service. The Lapland reindeer (upper left) is still used today as a draft and pack animal.

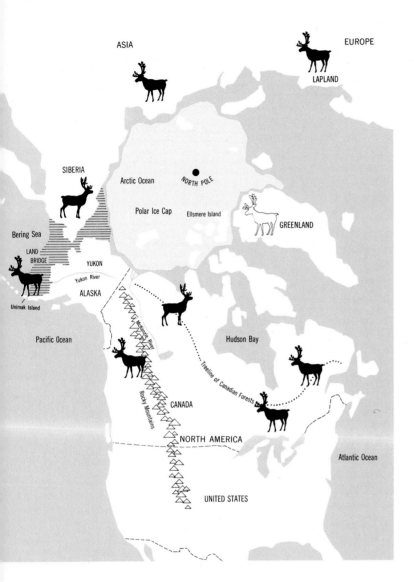

wolves which prey upon them, are as white as their icy homeland is.

Woodland caribou range through the evergreen forests of southern Canada from Newfoundland and Nova Scotia to the Rocky Mountains. Populations of this woodland race live in the Rockies and are the only caribou which wander south of the Canadian border into northern Idaho and Washington.

Barren ground caribou are famous for their long migrations in spring and fall. Larger and lighter in color than the woodland caribou, they blend well with the treeless plains where they spend part of each year. These animals range across northern Canada from the Mackenzie River to the Hudson Bay.

During April and May herds of barren ground caribou cows, followed by their yearlings, gather at the tree line. They are joined by other herds until thousands move northward to a thunder of clicking tendons. The bulls follow some weeks later, keeping separate from the cows, calves, and yearlings during most of the year.

Caribou look shaggy as they shed their winter coats. Their socks and neck-capes are covered with mud. They are attacked by hordes of flies and mosquitoes. But the long hard journey is worthwhile for the frozen plains of the Arctic tundra have now come to life. In brief summer, the top few inches of earth have thawed. During the long days and nights when the sun never sets, vegetation grows green and lush. Caribou find lichens, mosses, dwarf willow and birch trees, and small berry bushes on which they can browse.

In late May and early June the calves are born. They weigh between ten and 12 pounds. Within a few hours they are able to follow their mothers and after three days they can run faster than a man. They are nursed until the end of summer. By then they are eating the vegetation and weigh nearly 50 pounds.

By October the herds reach the tree line for the brief breeding season. The bulls lock antlers and fight to keep a harem of ten or 12 cows. Soon afterward they lose their antlers as the rutting time ends. The cows lose their antlers in the spring after calving.

Even farther south caribou were once abundant, where it is sufficiently cold and wooded. But in the early 1900s caribou disappeared because of hunting, logging, and forest fires. Soon all were gone from the United States, except those in Alaska and a small number in Idaho.

Caribou have since been introduced to Washington and Minnesota, and a few years ago a small herd was flown across the Canadian boundary onto Mt. Katahdin, Maine. Now thanks to such efforts, our North American reindeer are back.

Able to walk only hours after its birth, this caribou calf will soon join with the herd for their long migration.

Reindeer and Caribou Lands

*T*he first wild reindeer herds lived in northern Asia in what is now Siberia. From there they wandered east to Alaska and Canada, and west to northern and central Europe and to Greenland.

Scientists believe reindeer came to North America during the earth's long Ice Age. As the seawater froze to form glaciers, the level of the ocean dropped. A land bridge (see striped area) was formed in the Bering Sea between Siberia and Alaska. Reindeer and other animals were then able to cross to the North American continent.

The several different races of North American caribou are believed to belong to the same species as European reindeer.

Just as the Plains Indians depended on the buffalo, the Eskimos and Indians of Alaska and northern Canada based their way of life on the caribou. They did not tame caribou because they were hunters rather than herders. Caribou was an important target for them. In addition to food, its hides furnished clothing and tent coverings. Even the sinew was used for thread and the bones were carved into needles, knives, and spear points.

Animals of Bible and Song

When the rest of mankind perished by flood, the righteous Noah and his family were saved by Noah's obedience to God's command (Genesis 7:4-17). And wildlife's survival was ensured as the animals "went in two and two . . . into the ark, the male and the female. . . ."

Inspired by this Old Testament story, American folk artist Edward Hicks painted "Noah's Ark" in 1846.

An Ark Full of Cookies

Let wildlife be the motif for your Christmas cookies. Prepare a holiday treat for your entire family by baking a gingerbread ark filled with animal cookies. Let this festive creation serve as a reminder of man's concern for wildlife throughout history.

For instructions on how to fashion your own ark full of cookies, please turn page.

Gingerbread Noah's Ark

1½ cups shortening
1½ cups granulated sugar
2 cups light molasses
8½ cups unsifted all-purpose flour
1½ teaspoons baking soda
1½ teaspoons salt
4½ teaspoons ground ginger
1½ teaspoons nutmeg

Chocolate Icing, below

1. Melt shortening in medium saucepan. Stir in granulated sugar and molasses. Pour into a large bowl.

2. Sift 6 cups flour with the baking soda, salt and spices. Beat flour mixture, about one fourth at a time, into shortening mixture. Then, using hands, knead rest of flour into dough until thoroughly combined and smooth.

3. Divide dough in half. Wrap in foil, plastic wrap or waxed paper; then refrigerate dough for several hours or overnight.

4. Meanwhile, make patterns for sections of ark, as directed below.

5. Let dough stand at room temperature until you can roll it easily—20 to 30 minutes. Then, on two 17-by-14-inch cookie sheets, roll out each half of dough, covered with a sheet of waxed paper, to within ¼ inch of edge of cookie sheet all around.

6. Preheat oven to 275°F.

7. Place patterns for ark on top of waxed paper. Trace around pattern outlines with a sharp knife. Remove waxed paper. Leave dough trimmings in place on cookie sheets.

8. Bake 35 to 40 minutes. Cut around each section of ark; remove excess baked dough.

9. Let sections of ark cool, still on cookie sheets on wire racks, until cool and crisp.

10. Make Chocolate Icing. Assemble ark as directed below.

Chocolate Icing

1-lb pkg confectioners' sugar
2/3 cup regular unsweetened cocoa
½ cup egg whites (3)
½ teaspoon cream of tartar

1. In large bowl of electric mixer, combine confectioners' sugar, cocoa, egg whites and cream of tartar.

2. At low speed, beat until blended.

Then beat at high speed 5 minutes, or until icing forms stiff peaks when beater is slowly raised.

3. Cover bowl with damp paper towels if not to be used right away.

4. Set aside ½ cup of icing to use later for glaze on ark and animals. Use rest to construct ark and cabin and to decorate animals, as directed below.

To Make Patterns for Animals and Gingerbread Noah's Ark

Animals: On tissue paper, draw outline of each animal cookie, using cookies in photograph as a guide. Cut out. Trace outlines on cardboard or heavy paper; then cut out again. For snakes, roll a bit of dough between hands to make a roll 4 inches long. Arrange on

cookie sheet as pictured.

Noah's Ark: On tissue paper, draw an outline of each section of ark, as shown in diagrams. Cut out. Trace outlines on heavy paper; then cut again.

To Assemble Ark

1. Lay one ark end flat on right side. Pipe chocolate icing (in a pastry tube with number-8 writing tip) along edges. Set ark sides into icing and hold firmly several minutes.

2. Set ark with the small side down. Pipe icing along ends of sides; fit remaining ark end into icing. Prop sides with cans or cups. Pipe icing to seal all sides of each joint at corner of ark. Let dry until icing is hard—about 1 hour.

3. Assemble cabin walls and ends, using same method. Pipe icing along edges

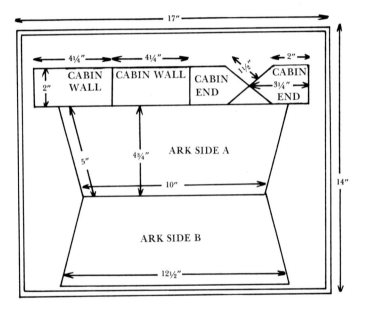

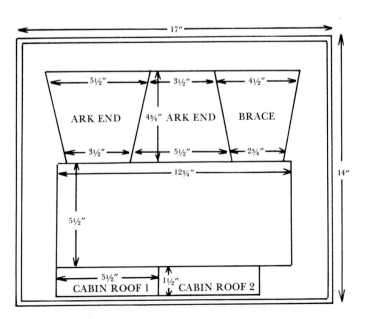

of points on cabin ends. Fit cabin roof (1) onto one side of points and cabin roof (2) onto other side. Pipe icing along edges of roof, to join them and form a ridgepole. Let dry until icing is hard—about 1 hour.

4. Pipe icing on edges of long sides of brace. Gently push small end of brace vertically between sides of ark, in center. Then pipe more icing on each side of brace, where it joins sides of the ark.

5. Pipe icing along top of sides and brace. Fit deck onto top of icing, pressing gently. Then pipe icing around edges of deck. Let dry until icing is hard—about 1 hour. Pipe icing along bottom edge of assembled cabin. Center on deck of ark. Set aside until thoroughly dry.

Animal Cookies

4 cups sifted (see Note) all-purpose flour
½ teaspoon salt
¾ cup butter or regular margarine, softened
1½ cups granulated sugar
2 eggs
1 teaspoon vanilla extract
¼ teaspoon almond extract

Patterns for animals, above
Icing for animals, below

1. Sift flour with salt onto waxed paper; set aside.

2. In large bowl of electric mixer, at medium speed, beat butter with granulated sugar until light and fluffy.

3. Add eggs, one at a time, beating well after each addition. Add vanilla and almond extracts.

4. At low speed, beat in flour mixture, a small amount at a time, blending well after each addition. Beat until smooth.

5. Preheat oven to 350°F.

6. Divide dough in half. On a lightly greased 17-by-14-inch cookie sheet, place half of dough. Roll dough, covered with a sheet of waxed paper, ⅛ inch thick.

7. Place animal patterns on top of waxed paper. Trace around pattern outlines with sharp knife. Remove waxed paper. Lift off dough trimmings and combine with remaining unrolled dough. (If dough seems soft, refrigerate 30 minutes, or until firm.)

8. Bake cookies 10 to 15 minutes, or until edges are lightly browned.

9. Remove to wire rack; let cool.

10. Repeat rolling and cutting rest of dough.

11. Meanwhile, make icing.

Icing for Animals

1-lb pkg confectioners' sugar, sifted
1/3 cup egg whites (3)
½ teaspoon cream of tartar
Blue, yellow, red and green food color

1. In large bowl of electric mixer, combine sugar, egg whites and cream of tartar.

2. At low speed, beat until blended. Then beat at high speed 5 minutes, or until icing forms stiff peaks when beater is slowly raised.

3. To decorate animals as shown: Reserve 1 cup of white; divide remaining frosting into four dishes and tint blue, yellow, pink and light green. Use as pictured; then add more color for the brighter shades. Use reserved Chocolate Icing where brown is needed. Frosting may be thinned with a few drops of water if necessary.

Makes about 2¼ cups—enough to decorate the 30 animal cookies.

To decorate: Using a spatula dipped in cold water, spread cookies with icing of appropriate color. Let dry. Then trim, as shown, with icing put through a pastry tube with a number-4 plain tip for writing. Use Chocolate Icing where needed. (See photograph.)

Makes 30 assorted animal cookies.

Note: Sift before measuring.

To Decorate Ark

2 oz almond paste (see Note)
Confectioners' sugar
8 almonds, 10 pecans

1. With hands, knead paste until workable.

2. Sprinkle board with confectioners' sugar; in it, roll almond paste into two small rolls 2¼ inches long. Use to outline windows in ark, as pictured. Brush backs with reserved Chocolate Icing and attach to cabin.

3. Roll out a 17-inch rope of almond paste to make scallop edge. Brush top of one ark side with Chocolate Icing. Decorate with almond-paste scallops, almonds and pecans, as pictured. Any remaining almond paste can be used to fasten animals to ark.

4. Brush roof of cabin with Chocolate Icing.

Note: Do not use commercial almond filling.

The Friendly Beasts

English -- Twelfth Century

Not too slow

mp

1. Je - sus, our broth - er, kind and good, Was hum - bly
2. "I," said the don - key, all shag - gy and brown, "I car - ried His

born in a sta - ble rude. The friend - ly beasts a -
moth - er up - hill and down, I car - ried her safe - ly to

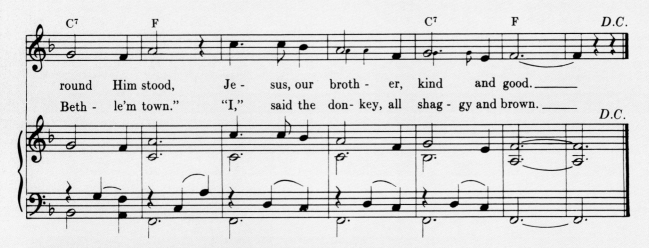

round Him stood, Je - sus, our broth- er, kind and good.____

Beth - le'm town." "I," said the don- key, all shag- gy and brown.____

D.C.

3

"I," said the cow, all white and red,
"I gave Him my manger for a bed,
I gave Him my hay to pillow His head."
"I," said the cow, all white and red.

4

"I," said the sheep with the curly horn,
"I gave Him my wool for a blanket warm,
He wore my coat on Christmas morn."
"I," said the sheep with the curly horn.

5

"I," said the dove from the rafters high,
"I cooed Him to sleep so He would not cry,
We cooed Him to sleep, my mate and I."
"I," said the dove from the rafters high.

6

So every beast, by some good spell,
In the stable rude was glad to tell
Of the gift he gave Immanuel,
The gift he gave Immanuel.

The Birds of Christmas

I know not what small winter birds these are,
Warbling their hearts out in that dusky glade
While the pale lustre of the morning star
   In heaven begins to fade.

Not me they sing for, this—earth's shortest—day,
A human listening at his window-glass;
They would, affrighted, cease and flit away
   At glimpse even of my face.

And yet how strangely mine their music seems,
As if of all things loved my heart was heir,
Had helped create them—albeit in my dreams—
   And they disdained my share.

Birds in Winter
—Walter de la Mare

The mockingbird—able to trill the melodies of other birds—provides year-round song throughout most of its range, even at night.

Winter Visitors and Year-round Friends

After birds wing south in the au-tumn, watching for the newly arrived—as well as for those that have stayed on—is a pleasant pastime.

"Heading south" means different things to dif-ferent species of birds. For while the brown creep-er of New England flies all the way to Florida, the Eider duck—which breeds mostly in Canada—con-siders the December-January weather of Massa-chusetts "tropical" enough.

Puzzling is the fact that birds may leave an area of abundance before there is any hint of cold. While some simply follow their food source, others respond to the changing proportion of light hours to dark. In recent years, a small number of migra-tory birds have changed their status to year-round residents. Ornithologists cite artificial feeding as a possible reason for the northern extension of win-ter and permanent ranges.

In Myakka River State Park near Sarasota, egrets enjoy Flor-ida's mild weather. Ample food, an abundance of water, and an agreeable climate entice some to stay through the year.

As the Days Grow Cold

W inter is a grim and bitter season for wild-life in our northern states and Canada. When it creeps across the land, the deer knows no bed for the snow, the fox must find food in a landscape buried beneath drifts, and the chickadee must roll with the punches of each bullying blast. Life in the wild reaches its lowest ebb.

But for all its deadly inclination, winter meets its match in the hardy birds and animals who call this north-land home. Fitted by design and instinct to thrive on adversity, they somehow manage to stay reasonably warm, find sufficient food, and escape predation and disease, each in his own way. And Man, feeling the sullen intrusion of cold in spite of civilization's trappings, marvels that any survive until spring; yet, this is part of the way of life.

Not all creatures fight it out with winter. Most birds migrate to warmer climates. Many insects lay eggs and then die. Frogs and turtles lie dormant in pond-bottom mud, and snakes curl up in underground crevices far below the frost line.

Many mammals take the easy way out by hibernating in caves and underground burrows. But only one lone race of birds, the poor-will, seems to enjoy hibernating. It nests from British Columbia to Mexico, then winters in the Southwest, where it has been found, on occasion, sleeping away the coldest days in California and Arizona.

What of those who carry on business as usual in the face of winter's worst, who neither migrate nor hibernate? First, they must possess an efficient means of retaining body heat. Mammals have fur to do this job. Birds have feathers to do it.

The ruffed grouse's pint-sized body is buried in a sumptuous layer of plumage. Visible ends of the contour feathers are sleek and smooth, but the concealed portions are densely downy. For added warmth each contour feather bears an "aftershaft"—a shorter downy feather that grows from the base of the main shaft. Like other birds, its feathers are "adjustable". In cold weather a resting grouse looks round as a puffball and twice her normal size because her feathers are raised to create a maximum of air spaces. In warm weather they are compressed or hang loosely to eliminate the insulating air. For additional ventilation many feathers are moulted after the spring breeding season and not replaced until fall.

Were it not for the insulating qualities of their feathers, great horned owls could not nest when they do—in the zero weather of late winter. But the eggs, surrounded by parted breast feathers and warmed by the bird's bare "brood patch", are kept safe from fatal chilling.

Feathers or fur are not always enough; most wild animals seek shelter of one form or another during colder

At home from the Gulf of Mexico to the Arctic, the great horned owl dares to nest long before spring. With keen ears and with eyes 100 times more sensitive to faint light than man's, it tracks down small rodents for itself and its young.

months. Even those tireless roamers—the weasels, the mink and the otter—usually have winter dens in which to take at least temporary refuge. And that fresh-air fiend, the red fox, often has a hole handy in case a storm or sudden danger should strike.

But what about birds? They like to sleep warm too. Several times I've found flocks of two hundred or more evening grosbeaks roosting among dense clusters of dead leaves clinging to small oak trees in a wooded lowland. The birds snuggled into the thickest bunches of leaves in late afternoon and quietly awaited darkness. Screech owls commonly snooze away the day in hollow trees and abandoned flicker or pileated woodpecker's nest holes. In fact, most cavity nesters sleep in tree cavities in winter.

Loose. snow itself is a good insulator. Ruffed grouse commonly fly headlong into deep snow to spend the night or sleep out a storm. A nocturnal snowfall often covers the entrance hole, and many a hiker has been set back on his heels by a grouse suddenly bursting out of the unbroken whiteness like a jet-propelled snowblower.

Survival in winter involves more than merely retaining body heat. Finding food to produce the heat in the first place is essential, and not easy when snow lies several feet deep, and ice covers many lakes and streams. But the ruffed grouse survives the winter months more painlessly than most.

Much of the grouse's success is due to its ability to utilize a variety of foods that are always available. During the summertime it eats insects, greens and berries, gradually turning to more mast, seeds and wild fruits as autumn progresses. When snow covers most of these foods it merely shifts to a diet of buds, upon which it can live exclusively all winter if necessary. Buds are a food snows cannot hide; only an ice storm can make them unavailable to the enterprising grouse.

The goshawk (above), a large bird of prey that specializes in hunting grouse, occasionally wanders from its northern forest home in search of food when winter comes. So, too, may the pine grosbeak (below), frequently sighted by alpine skiers.

The pileated woodpecker (left), satisfied with carpenter ants in local woods, feels no great need to roam.

The dead of winter would seem to be a difficult period for insectivorous birds, but a small group—the woodpeckers, nuthatches and creepers—get through the winter eating little but insect life. And it's surprising where they find such food. Adult and immature insects and their eggs are picked from crevices in the bark, while many larvae are chiseled out of the wood itself. Woodpeckers visit fields to find borers in the cornstalks. Chickadees peck open praying mantis egg cases and eat the newly hatched baby mantises. Champion insect-extractor is the big pileated woodpecker. No borer tunnels deeply enough into the heartwood of a tree to escape him. I've seen his rectangular excavations—some large enough to hold a shoe box—and the piles of chips that litter the snow and clearly understand why the "cock-of-the-woods" has no serious competitor.

As scarce as food can be in our northern states, it is sometimes more scarce above the Canadian border. Goshawks, those splendid predators of the northern forests, wander farther south in winter in search of prey, showing up in northern states which normally do not have a breeding population of these birds. Snowy owls leave their tundra home when lemmings—their principal food—undergo one of their recurring periods of scarcity.

Evening grosbeaks, breeding for the most part in Canada's spruce forests and the mountains of the West and Northwest, have extended their winter range into northeastern United States—originally in search of more abundant seeds, wild fruits and similar fare, but recently spurred by fond memories of sunflower seeds in backyard bird feeders, I suspect. Also pine grosbeaks, crossbills, and other finches of Canada may invade the northern states.

Most fish-eating birds move south when ice threatens to cover their feeding places, but where open water remains you will sometimes find a few American mergansers spending the winter, diving in the frigid water to snatch small fish in their saw-toothed bills. Hardy old squaw and goldeneye ducks often keep them company, feeding chiefly on crustaceans and aquatic insect life. With waterproof plumage and big feet for diving, these hardy birds can obtain enough food to survive the winter.

The ruffed grouse, who seeks his food on land, is lucky. Each fall he acquires "snowshoes." Tiny scales along the margins of the toes begin to lengthen, and by the first snowfall they form a comblike fringe that doubles the area of each toe. When warmer days reduce the deepest drifts, the fringe drops from the grouse's foot unnoticed.

For some, spring comes too late. In every wildlife species individuals have paid with their lives for flaws and weaknesses that could not stand the test of cold and hunger. Nature is called cruel, but in her impartiality she endlessly repeats the process by which the fittest survive, their kind increase, and life-saving adaptations are born, forced by the long, hard, cold winter.

Ned Smith

Each year a number of birds which breed in our country spend a sunny Christmas "South of the Border" in either South or Central America or the West Indies.

The Baltimore—or Northern—oriole (left) winters in Mexico, Central America, and Colombia. When mating time nears, it will fly back to North America to settle in the temperate climate east of the Rockies.

Joining thousands of other martins, the purple martin (below) navigates its way to Brazil every August. It will not return to the United States until the following April. Though its departure and arrival dates are somewhat later, the rose-breasted grosbeak (bottom left) is also an annual South American vacationer.

While indigo buntings (top left) are in Mexico, Cuba, or Panama, they undergo their second molt of the year—shedding their pale feathers of autumn. By the time spring arrives, they sport brilliant blue.

Other cold-weather visitors to Latin America are the chimney swift, the veery, the scarlet tanager, and many members of the warbler family. But of all our migrants, the champion is the Arctic tern. After breeding in Alaska, it flies halfway around the world to catch "summer" at the opposite pole.

111

"And a Partridge in a Pear Tree"

In the well-loved carol "The 12 Days of Christmas", which celebrates the season's custom of giving and receiving, six of the gifts named are birds.

Partridges, French hens, turtledoves, geese, and swans are all familiar to most of us. But what of the song's strange-sounding colly bird? It is simply a black bird—the word "colly" being associated with coal dust or soot.

Both the bobwhite quail (right), and the ruffed grouse (above) were mistakenly referred to as "partridges" by this country's early colonists who were homesick for familiar wildlife. A winter favorite, the grouse adapts unusually well to cold weather. When snows come, they often perch in orchard trees, nibbling on the dormant buds which are an important item in their diet. Once called "fool hens" because they were easily hunted, today's birds are more wary. In contrast to the grouse which can scratch through the snow's crust to find food, bobwhite are helpless and suffer a high cold-weather mortality rate.

"True" partridges were imported to this country by sportsmen in the late 1800s. Released, the birds have subsequently bred. The gray, or Hungarian, partridge and the chukar partridge are now considered important gamebirds in some of our northern and western states.

In 18th century England, the song on the following pages was a children's game of memory and forfeits. Can you name all the gifts of the day without looking?

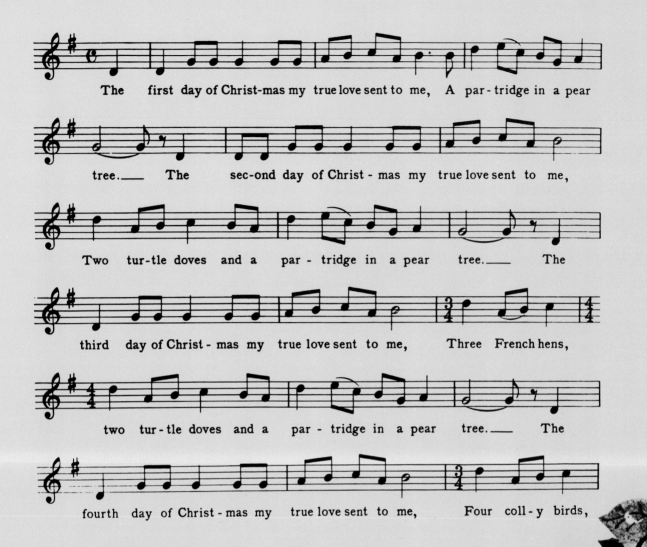

The first day of Christ-mas my true love sent to me, A par-tridge in a pear tree.___ The sec-ond day of Christ-mas my true love sent to me, Two tur-tle doves and a par-tridge in a pear tree.___ The third day of Christ-mas my true love sent to me, Three French hens, two tur-tle doves and a par-tridge in a pear tree.___ The fourth day of Christ-mas my true love sent to me, Four coll-y birds,

Twelve Days of Christmas

Six geese a‑lay‑ing,
Sev‑en swans a‑swim‑ming (six *etc.*)
Eight maids a‑milk‑ing (seven *etc.*)
Nine la‑dies danc‑ing (eight *etc.*)
Ten lords a‑leap‑ing (nine *etc.*)
Elev‑en pi‑pers pi‑ping (ten *etc.*)
Twelve drum‑mers drum‑ming (eleven *etc.*)

three French hens, two tur-tle doves and a par-tridge in a pear

tree.___ The fifth day of Christ-mas my true love sent to me,

Five gold___ rings, Four coll-y birds, three French hens,

two___ tur-tle doves and a par-tridge in a pear tree. *etc.*

Living and Dining Al Fresco

Summer or winter, birds which fish from the sea—such as the puffin and gull—always find food plentiful. But for many birds who live off the land, discovering a good meal in the coldest months of the year is not so simple.

Tree swallows and flycatchers, who dine on insects, head south as cold weather imprisons their food source. The barred and screech owls are permanent residents but find the variety of their winter menu limited as many rodents and other small mammals go into hiding. Forest birds—pine siskins, evening grosbeaks, and crossbills—leave their breeding grounds to flock to our gardens in search of food.

When snow covers dried berries and ice sheaths the seed pods, fruit and seed eaters like the English sparrow find hunger knocking. At times like this, a bag of suet or a mixture of wild bird seed at the feeder shows that we care about our winged wildlife.

The Atlantic puffin, which winters as far south as Massachusetts, is an excellent fisherman. After a successful trip, it may return with up to 11 fish in its beak.

The cold seldom bothers New England's hardy junco, or snow-
bird, as flocks numbering 100 or more come and go all winter.

The Night of the Snowbirds

It was a few minutes past four o'clock on December 21, the shortest day of the year, and the thermometer read five below zero as I stood in the yard outside my room in Ann Arbor, Michigan. A graduate biology student, I had a special cold-weather survival study to do for Professor Harry W. Hann, the renowned ornithologist: my assignment was to find a roosting bird and observe it every hour on the hour throughout the night. Now in the crackling cold twilight I scouted the vines for house sparrows, the brushy edges of the yard for cardinals, the pony barn for starlings—without success. The shortest day meant the longest night and the birds, wherever they were, had apparently gone to bed early.

Then suddenly a gust of wind shot around the corner of the house and blew into my life a flock of snowbirds—pirouetting on the frigid breeze, they began dropping gaily to the snow in the lee of the building, tossing their heads and calling wistfully to each other—*"Zill, zill . . . zill, zill"*. Dark on the head and upper body, with white underplumage, they looked like little monks in gray cowls and white surplices. I scribbled my first note: "Twenty snowbirds (slate-colored juncos) , hopping up and down, scratching snow with both feet together. Doubt they're finding food, snow too deep. Three of them inspecting sumac bush in shelter of pony barn as possible roost. Could be a good place."

So began my long night of the snowbirds. At that moment I had no way of knowing that the next 15 hours were going to cost me my heart as well as what I had come to think of as my "scientific attitude;" but I remember I had vague premonitions, a feeling of foreboding, almost of dread. Southern Michigan was in the grip of a six-day cold snap with intermittent blizzards, conditions that had often wiped out vast numbers of birds in the past. Also I was suffering a touch of nervousness for this was my first invitation to contribute to a professional work in progress, a paper on how birds survive in killing cold. I recalled the words of Dr. Hann. "It won't be easy. . . . The hard thing is to remain objective, detached. No food handouts, for instance." He winked, but he meant it.

In the next minutes the birds took over the dense sumac bushes, hopping in and out from the branches to the snow. I tried to recall what I knew about them. Not very much, except that my uncle in Pennsylvania always said that when the snowbirds came early he laid in an extra cord of wood—to him, their arrival meant that the cap of the globe was already iced and spring would be late, for he considered snowbirds the harbingers of cold weather, and the earlier they arrived, the longer the winter.

By 4:30 darkness was closing in. Pained by cold, I stepped inside and stacked on my desk the reference books I would want through the night. Snowbirds, I discovered, are members of the sparrow family, whose cousins include the grosbeaks, cardinals, pine siskins and crossbills. Each of the groups has a beak adapted to opening different kinds of seeds. The beak of the crossbill can pry pinecones apart. The cardinal has a heavy beak which cracks sturdy seeds. The snowbird's delicate beak is used for snapping grass seeds from their sheaths.

When I stepped out on the porch again, it was almost dark; but the light from my window fell on . . . the birds jostling for positions. Social birds like snowbirds roost according to their status, particularly on cold nights, the oldest and biggest . . . demanding the best site—the area best protected from wind and predator—usually in the center of the group. The young and weak are pushed to the dangerous edges.

Suddenly one of the roosting birds flew down from the sumac, alighted and opened his feathers to the snow. With flips and beats he spun the crystals into his breast, then dipped his head into the snow . . . I returned to my desk and checked a reference on "snow bathing"—it is done, apparently, to make their feathers lie more smoothly, thereby creating a sleek windbreaker. Several other birds flew down and joined the first—they flipped the snow over themselves and returned to their twigs to snap their feathers into alignment—an important job this night, which the birds seemed to sense for they preened busily for nine or ten minutes.

The final ritual of going to bed was delightful. "Much adjusting of feet," I wrote. "There is 'talking' and wing threatening. One bird settles down nicely then gets up and moves over toward his neighbor who warns him off with a drooping of his wings." Thus they arrive at a "comfort zone" for each individual: . . . separate, yet close enough to share radiant heat from the group.

Birds can express anxiety so I tried to count the good-night chirps as some sort of barometer of their concern . . . "The calls are frequent and sharp," I wrote. I did not add . . . that they seemed to grow more plaintive as the thermometer dropped and the sky blackened.

At twenty to five the voices ceased abruptly. According to authorities, this was because a degree of darkness had been reached that had tripped a switch in their internal machinery and put them to sleep. With this silence they began their fight to survive the longest and . . . coldest night of the year. They were prepared for it. Snowbirds lay down a layer of fat for the winter and although they do not eat as much in winter as in summer, they weigh more. The fat usually . . . insulates and is burned to provide heat. Without an abundant food supply to regain weight promptly, the birds die of starvation. These birds had been hard put to find food for several days.

Suddenly the night was upon us; cold, gripping and promising storm. But I hesitated to go in for I still did not have an individual bird to watch, as Professor Hann required. I went closer to the sumac bush, and as I did so, a small snowbird—one of those pushed to the vulnerable outside of the group—leaned down into the light from the window and eyed me. Male or female I could not tell, but "he" came more naturally. His head was soft, his eyelids were half-lifted in bird drowsiness. His breast feathers were fluffed to hold his body heat. I focused my binoculars to see more clearly. A white tip on his beak—a touch of albinism or an old injury—marked him from all others. I had my individual. As a watched him pull one slender foot into his feathers, a name came to mind—"Zill", the last good-night note of the snowbird.

At the six o'clock check, tree limbs cracked as they froze around us. Zill was still on one foot. I wondered why it did not freeze. The feet of winter songbirds, I learned from paging through books, have a reduced blood supply, so there is very little liquid to freeze. Futhermore the scales in the legs and toes are made from tissues similar to our hair and nails, which are not affected by temperature.

The next several hourly observations were reassuring. "Zill shifting feet and moving. Struck neighbor. Neighbor struck back. Niko Tinbergen says this activity keeps birds' temperatures up." The stimulation of the whack together with the anger that follows circulates the blood, and raises the body temperature. At ten o'clock I noted that Zill had put his head in the feathers of his back. "This is good," I commented. "He is balled so tightly that he has very lit-

This mallard drake and his hens—in search of aquatic weeds —represent our country's most abundant duck. On freezing days they find the open water warmer than the air around it.

tle surface area from which to lose heat. Also keeps what he has, by breathing it back into his feathers." . . .

Two biological laws of the wild—Bergmann's Law and Allen's Law—illustrate further what the bird was doing. Some northern species of animals and birds—the snow-shoe rabbits, for instance—have large bodies and small legs, ears and tails, creating a "ball-like" animal with little surface area from which to lose heat. On the other hand, a southern species such as the desert jackrabbit, has long ears, legs and body from which to lose heat and keep cool.

As the night wore slowly on, the temperature continued to drop and it started to snow. To quiet my fears I studied references on how other birds spent cold nights. Their arrangements seemed less perilous than the snowbirds'. Chickadees, woodpeckers, and nuthatches go into holes in trees, and these holes are heated by the birds to somewhere around a cozy 70 degrees Fahrenheit. Ducks stayed right on the water in subzero nights, so that they would float in the warmest environment of all—the 32-degree water. Pigeons and starlings often seek the ledges of concrete buildings that have soaked in sunlight all day and still retain some heat. Quail actually touch bodies to keep warm on cold nights, sitting in a circle (heads out to detect danger), while grosbeaks use another source of radiant energy. They reflect their own body warmth from the dried leaves that often remain all winter on beech and oak. Grosbeaks sit close to these shields. Haystacks and haylofts shelter hundreds of sparrows and finches.

At midnight, . . . the temperature now read 19 below, the snow was falling steadily, and the birds were hauntingly quiet. My handwriting was worried and small. "Subject quivering. He moved closer to his neighbor. Snow blowing through keyhole of my door."

This was when I began really to fear the birds would not survive the night. In the *American Wildlife and Plants—A Guide to Food Habits*, by the United States Fish and Wildlife Service, I reread with despair the list of seeds the snowbirds eat. Panic-grass, crabgrass, violets and smartweeds—all long since buried. I felt somewhat encouraged when I recognized taller plants on the list—bristlegrass, goosefoot, timothy, ragweed, broomsedge and sumac. But I had already noted there were no berries on the sumac by the pony barn. I dozed on my arm until one o'clock.

The snow was blowing densely now. I got a brief glimpse of Zill crouched on his twig, his head lowered into the storm. "I think he is suffering," I wrote unrestrainedly. "He's puffed too much, like the Bowen's canary before it died of pneumonia. The snow is almost touching his feet."

At two I heard an alarm call from one of the birds in the sumac. I stepped out the door, but I could not see what was wrong—the snow had drifted thickly into the bush. I wondered why the fright and turned to the books again. A paper by animal behaviorist David E. Davis was not reassuring. Any potential harmful situation in the environment, he wrote, "will bring first an alarm reaction, then a stage of resistance or adaptation and finally—if the stressor persists—exhaustion and death." One of the stressors listed was "cold".

In a moment of sudden, overwhelming panic, I phoned another graduate student . . . to ask what to do. The phone rang on, unanswered. . . . [I thought of my heat lamp with an extension cord to reach the birds, and glanced despairingly into the bushes]. The sumac was almost covered. Not a wing fluttered to say the birds were alive. "I guess I don't need it," I said [to myself].

At four the radio announced that the snow was abating and the temperature had risen a degree. I opened the door and decided to go look for small bodies buried in the sumac. Perhaps I could revive a couple of them by holding them in my hand as I had done one spring to a cold, dying nestling. But suddenly a sense of hopelessness overwhelmed me: I did not go near the sumac bush. I shoved my notes into a folder and, setting the alarm for daybreak, fell asleep on the couch with my clothes on.

Morning at last. I awoke before it went off. Gray light misted the window and the frog pond cracked like a gun-shot in the cold. Reluctantly I went to the door—the wind had died but the snow had drifted thick in the lee of the barn. To put off the inevitable close inspection, I began shoveling the porch; and as I did so, the snow over the sumac burst open like a milkweed pod and out into the dark dawn flew the snowbirds! They flashed their white tail feathers, turned, wheeled and came down right beside the porch where I was standing. I stared, still not daring to believe. One of the birds had a beak tipped with white!

And then, in the midst of my relief and joy, I realized I had something valuable to report. In those days little was known about the natural insulating properties of snow and here I had observed an instance of it! While the trees snapped and the bottom fell out of the thermometer, the night itself had softly covered the birds with a warm blanket. It was light and air-filled, and the birds had breathed in it, making small insulated igloos with their bodies and breath.

Whatever remained of my scientific detachment left me in that moment. I dashed inside, collected chunks of bread, a bag of wild birdseed, suet and raisins. I tossed them abundantly. As the snowbirds swept down on my offerings, I laughed and called aloud, "Merry Christmas!" The birds spun white crystals into the cold air, the sun broke through the gray sky in the east and the long night of the snowbirds was done. "Merry Christmas," I said again; and with these words the birds wheeled around the corner of the house and disappeared.

Jean George

Feeders that invite birds to your yard offer not only a snack for the birds, but hours of entertainment for you. The evening grosbeaks (above) are attracted by sunflower seeds. Many other birds, including cardinals, purple finches, and crossbills, are sunflower seed fans, too.

For the downy woodpecker (left) and for chickadees and nuthatches, suet provides a heat-energy meal similar to our steak and potatoes. Congealed pan drippings or fat trimmed from meat can be stuffed into net bags or into holes drilled in a small log, and should be suspended far enough from the ground to discourage frisky dogs. If the suet is finely ground, nearly all birds love it.

In watching the birds you will soon discover that individual tastes differ. Like people, some blue jays and starlings like mashed potatoes—others can't stand them. For fun, try serving kitchen leftovers and see who will come to dinner.

123

Most of the time wildlife can fend for itself and doesn't need to be fed by man. But in severe winter weather, when ice and snow make food hard to find, birds are grateful for handouts. The important thing to remember is that once you start the feeding, you should continue it. Otherwise, those that have come to depend on you as a reliable food source might possibly starve.

Perched on a handmade wooden tray, the male cardinal (below) eyes an assortment of favorite seeds. Along with juncos, grackles, song sparrows, and others, the cardinal also enjoys toast and finely ground cookie crumbs.

Many birds love fruit. Berries frozen from summer will lure mockingbirds, catbirds, hermit thrushes, and bluebirds.

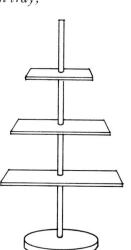

Feeders can be as plain or as ornate as you wish. The festive one attracting goldfinches (far left) was made from less than a yard of trellis wood, and a dowel. The tree was held upright by imbedding it in a mixture of plaster of paris and water. Suet and seed were spread on the branches as a Christmas offering. The birds considered the tree such a treat its designer left it up until spring.

The pygmy nuthatch (below) enjoys peanut butter smeared on a digger pinecone, while the chickadee (left) makes a meal of doughnuts. Berries, popcorn, and peanuts strung together also prove very inviting.

Many birds, including sparrows and juncos, will eat off the ground in the absence of a feeder. But remember to make sure that the scattered seed is near some trees that offer a safe retreat. Otherwise, it might be your cat who will end up with the Christmas feast.

65290

Beginning a decade ago, we have trapped and banded most of the chickadees on our farm each winter. . . . 65290 was one of 7 chickadees constituting the 'class of 1937.' When he first entered our trap, he showed no visible evidence of genius. Like his classmates, his valor for suet was greater than his discretion. Like his classmates, he bit my finger while being taken out of the trap. When banded and released he fluttered up to a limb, pecked his new aluminum anklet in mild annoyance, shook his mussed feathers, cursed gently, and hurried away to catch up with the gang. It is doubtful whether he drew any philosophical deductions from his experience (such as 'all is not ants' eggs that glitters'), for he was caught again three times that same winter.

By the second winter our recaptures showed that the class of 7 had shrunk to 3, and by the third winter to 2. By the fifth winter 65290 was the sole survivor of his generation. Signs of genius were still lacking, but of his extraordinary capacity for living, there was now historical proof.

During his sixth winter 65290 failed to reappear, and the verdict of 'missing in action' is now confirmed by his absence during four subsequent trappings. At that, of 97 chicks banded during the decade, 65290 was the only one contriving to survive for five winters. Three reached 4 years, 7 reached 3 years, 19 reached 2 years, and 67 disappeared after their first winter. Hence if I were selling insurance to chicks, I could compute the premium with assurance. But this would raise the problem: in what currency would I pay the widows? I suppose in ants' eggs.

I know so little about birds that I can only speculate on why 65290 survived his fellows. Was he more clever in dodging his enemies? What enemies? A chickadee is almost too small to have any. That whimsical fellow called Evolution, having enlarged the dinosaur until he tripped over his own toes, tried shrinking the chickadee until he was just too big to be snapped up by flycatchers as an insect, and just too little to be pursued by hawks and owls as meat. Then he regarded his handiwork and laughed. Everyone laughs at so small a bundle of large enthusiasms.

The sparrow hawk, the screech owl, the shrike, and especially the midget saw-whet owl might find it worthwhile to kill a chickadee, but I've only once found evidence of actual murder: a screech-owl pellet contained one of my bands. Perhaps these small bandits have a fellow-feeling for midgets.

It seems likely that weather is the only killer so devoid of both humor and dimension as to kill a chickadee. I sus-

pect that in the chickadee Sunday School two mortal sins are taught: thou shalt not venture into windy places in winter, thou shalt not get wet before a blizzard.

I learned the second commandment one drizzly winter dusk while watching a band of chicks going to roost in my woods. The drizzle came out of the south, but I could tell it would turn northwest and bitter cold before morning. The chicks went to bed in a dead oak, the bark of which had peeled and warped into curls, cups, and hollows of various sizes, shapes, and exposures. The bird selecting a roost dry against a south drizzle, but vulnerable to a north one, would surely be frozen by morning. The bird selecting a roost dry from all sides would awaken safe. This, I think, is the kind of wisdom that spells survival in chickdom, and accounts for 65290 and his like.

The chickadee's fear of windy places is easily deduced from his behavior. In winter he ventures away from woods only on calm days, and the distance varies inversely as the breeze. I know several windswept woodlots that are chickless all winter, but are freely used at all other seasons. They are windswept because cows have browsed out the undergrowth. To the steam-heated banker who mortgages the farmer who needs more cows who need more pasture, wind is a minor nuisance, except perhaps at the Flatiron corner. To the chickadee, winter wind is the boundary of the habitable world. If the chickadee had an office, the maxim over his desk would say: 'Keep calm.'

His behavior at the trap discloses the reason. Turn your trap so that he must enter with even a moderate wind at his tail, and all the king's horses cannot drag him to the bait. Turn it the other way, and your score may be good. Wind from behind blows cold and wet under the feathers, which are his portable roof and air-conditioner. Nuthatches, juncos, tree sparrows, and woodpeckers likewise fear winds from behind, but their heating plants and hence their wind tolerance are larger in the order named. Books on nature seldom mention wind; they are written behind stoves.

I suspect there is a third commandment in chickdom: thou shalt investigate every loud noise. When we start chopping in our woods, the chicks at once appear and stay until the felled tree or riven log has exposed new insect eggs or pupae for their delectation. The discharge of a gun will likewise summon chicks, but with less satisfactory dividends. . . .

65290 has long since gone to his reward. I hope that in his new woods, great oaks full of ants' eggs keep falling all day long, with never a wind to ruffle his composure or take the edge off his appetite. And I hope that he still wears my band.

Aldo Leopold

The black-capped chickadee both nests and winters in the northern half of the United States and in southern Canada. During cold weather it consumes insect eggs hidden in tree bark.

Who Killed Cock Robin?

*Cock Robin's death was only
a nursery fable—not so the pesticides
the author fears.*

There was once a town in the heart of America where all life seemed to live in harmony with its surroundings. The town lay in the midst of a checkerboard of prosperous farms, with fields of grain and hillsides of orchards where, in spring, white clouds of bloom drifted above the green fields. In autumn, oak and maple and birch set up a blaze of color that flamed and flickered across a backdrop of pines. . . .

Along the roads, laurel, viburnum and alder, great ferns and wildflowers delighted the traveler's eye through much of the year. Even in winter the roadsides were places of beauty, where countless birds came to feed on the berries and on the seed heads of the dried weeds rising above the snow. The countryside was, in fact, famous for the abundance and variety of its bird life, and when the flood of migrants was pouring through in spring and fall people traveled from great distances to observe them. Others came to fish the streams, which flowed clear and cold out of the hills and contained shady pools where trout lay. So it had been from the days many years ago when the first settlers raised their houses. . . .

Then a strange blight crept over the area and everything began to change. Some evil spell had settled on the community: mysterious maladies swept the flocks of chickens; the cattle and sheep sickened and died. Everywhere was a shadow of death. The farmers spoke of much illness among their families. In the town the doctors had become more and more puzzled by new kinds of sickness appearing among their patients. There had been several sudden and unexplained deaths, not only among adults but even among children, who would be stricken suddenly while at play and die within a few hours.

There was a strange stillness. The birds, for example—where had they gone? . . . The feeding stations in the backyards were deserted. The few birds seen anywhere were moribund; they trembled violently and could not fly. It was a spring without voices. On the mornings that had once throbbed with the dawn chorus of robins, catbirds, doves, jays, wrens, and scores of other bird voices there was now no sound; only silence lay over the fields and woods and marsh.

On the farms the hens brooded, but no chicks hatched. The farmers complained that they were unable to raise any pigs—the litters were small and the young survived only a few days. The apple trees were coming into bloom but no bees droned among the blossoms, so there was no pollination and there would be no fruit.

The roadsides, once so attractive, were now lined with browned and withered vegetation as though swept by fire. These, too, were silent, deserted by all living things. Even the streams were now lifeless. Anglers no longer visited them, for all the fish had died.

In the gutters under the eaves and between the shingles of the roofs, a white granular powder still showed a few patches; some weeks before it had fallen like snow upon the roofs and the lawns, the fields and streams.

No witchcraft, no enemy action had silenced the rebirth of new life in this stricken world. The people had done it themselves. . . .

Rachel Carson

Bygone Greetings

Though it is hard to imagine Christmas without the exchange of cards, the custom is surprisingly little more than a century old. The first Christmas card was designed in England in 1843. Thirty-one years later production was begun in America by Louis Prang—four of whose popular bird designs are shown on these pages.

May Your Christmas be happy

A MERRY CHRISTMAS TO YOU!

"IT'S A POOR HEART THAT NEVER REJOICES."

A MERRY CHRISTMAS

YE CAROL.

Merry birds bear the Christmas Greeting

This owl quartette has come to cheer   May it be happy, every minute,
The   opening of the glad New Year.   With no false notes or discords in it.

Wildlife—long associated with

Christmas traditions—was used as a card mo-

tif not only by Prang, but later by

Wirths Bros. & Owen, whose delight-

ful "owls in a snowstorm" is shown opposite.

Deck the Halls for One and All

Long before Christmas was first celebrated in Europe, evergreen trees and plants were treasured as symbols of continuing life. With them, people decorated home and temple at the time of the winter solstice, when the northern hemisphere is tilted farthest from the sun. They prayed then that the sun might return from its flight into darkness—or rejoiced in its triumph over night, for triumph it always did, bringing more spring-like minutes of light and warmth each day.

Today, with many of the same greens we celebrate Christmas—a few days after the winter solstice—as we too rejoice in continuing life.

Of all the plants of winter, none is quite so special as the evergreen tree trimmed for Christmas. A white-footed mouse has discovered the hand-strung popcorn on this one. On another will be angel hair, commemorating the legend of the house spider whose silvery web adorned a poor family's tree.

Living Ornaments

The winter berries light the woods and the roadside, unusually numerous and altogether festive. They garland the woods, and black alders make a gay display of vivid red along the roadside—holly red, for the black alder is . . . cousin of the familiar Christmas holly.

Flowering dogwoods bore many berries, most of which were stripped early, as always, by the eager squirrels. And the birds soon stripped the big crop of pokeberries and woodbine. Even the poison ivy had a fruitful season, which means only that the birds will plant more of the noxious vines along the old stone walls.

Deeper in the woods, the lesser berry plants had a good season too. The baneberries . . . bore heavily and many of them still have their vivid berries. Checkerberry, the little plant with the big name, Gaultheria procumbens, and the tang of wintergreen and black birch, dangles its fat cherry-red fruits beneath its small canopy of evergreen leaves. And the trailing partridgeberry . . . seems to have been more fruitful than in years.

Some say the small berry plants, and the partridgeberry in particular, forecast the coming winter. Many berries, runs the belief, mean a cold, snowy season. The reasoning is backward, of course; many berries simply mean a favorable fruiting season just past. But there they stand—there they creep, rather, in the woodland beside the creeping pine and the Christmas fern, their berries like glossy little beads to decorate a tiny Christmas tree. Whatever the winter, partridges and their kind will have good eating. . . .

Hal Borland

While the holly (opposite left) was known and revered by the early Druids and Romans, recent cultivation produced the poinsettia (right)—once a small and unimposing Mexican weed.

The Plants and Flowers of Christmas

Many plants in the Christmas tradition are dear to us, but the four that have earned a very special place in our hearts are the holly and mistletoe of the Old World, and the poinsettia and Christmas cactus of the New. Of these, perhaps the most intriguing is mistletoe, blessed by the pagans and blasted by the church. According to one Scandinavian myth, Hoder (God of Winter) slew Balder (God of Light and Spring) with an arrow made of mistletoe wood. The tears of Balder's mother, Frigga, became the plant's berries. When the God of Light and Spring was revived, Frigga—in her joy—kissed everyone who passed beneath the mistletoe.

The Druids of ancient Britain used mistletoe to cure many ills, as did the Indians of America. The latter chewed its leaves to lessen the pain of toothache. In recent years a drug derived from mistletoe is said to lower blood pressure.

A parasite, mistletoe grows on a great variety of host trees in the South, Southwest, and Rocky Mountains. Winter birds, fond of its berries, help to "plant" the vine as they clean their bills on the branches of the trees.

The Christmas plant that traditionally brings the gladdest tidings is the holly. In ancient Rome holly wreaths were sent to newly married couples to express congratulations and goodwill. Like other peoples, the Romans believed that holly warded off evil spirits. In England, it protected against witches, mad dogs, and wild beasts. Christmas in London saw every house, church, street corner, and marketplace decorated with it.

Upon discovering holly in America, the early settlers were overjoyed to find a touch of "home" in the new land. But they might not have been quite so happy when they discovered how important the holly was to the natives. The Indians of Pennsylvania used it as a badge of courage; the Indians of New Jersey used the wood for tomahawk handles; and tribes to the south drank holly tea to give them strength.

Holly grows naturally in Europe, Asia, Africa, North America, and South America. At one time, wild holly was found from the coast of Massachusetts to Florida, extending inland as far as Texas and parts of the Middle West. Today it grows in abundance only in the low-lying coastal areas of the Southeast. An amazing characteristic of the holly tree is that some are male, others female. The female alone bears berries and will be fertile only if insects—or a lucky wind—bring pollen from the flowers of the male tree.

The Christmas cactus is an air plant which blooms in its native habitat—the mountains of Rio de Janeiro, Brazil—around Christmastime. Its flowers, ranging in color from white to crimson, crown arching green branches in a fountain of Christmas colors. As a houseplant, it must be given special care if it is to bloom in December. During its fall budding period, keep the cactus in a cool place. (A basement with a night temperature of 50 to 55 degrees is ideal.) It needs sunlight, but must also have at least 14 hours of darkness or its cycle of bloom will not produce Christmas flowers.

Our most unusual Christmas plant is the poinsettia we inherited from our Mexican neighbors. A poor girl, it is said, picked a flowering weed along the roadside to offer to the Virgin Mary. The moment she placed it before the statue in the church, the tiny plant burst into brilliant bloom. In Central America it is called "Flame Leaf" or "Flower of the Holy Night." "Flame Leaf" is the better name, for the brilliant flowers we admire are not really flowers at all. They are special leaves called bracts. These are usually red, but at times are white or slightly yellow.

About 150 years ago, Dr. Joel R. Poinsett, a botanist and our first ambassador to Mexico, brought the plant to his greenhouses in Greenville, South Carolina. He gave some to his friends and some to botanical gardens in the East. In the early 1900s Albert Ecke and his sons, of Hollywood, California, along with other flower producers, developed and popularized the plant. The poinsettia flourishes in tropical and subtropical regions, and therefore is popular in the Southeast and in southern California— where it may grow to be ten feet tall. A potted plant, however, will usually reach only two to four feet in height.

Providing your poinsettia with approximately the same conditions it had in the greenhouse, will help it thrive during the Christmas holidays. If it receives plenty of sunlight, is kept out of cold drafts, and watered regularly, it should retain its elegant beauty even after the season has passed. In June, move the plant to a sunny part of the garden. Bring it indoors before the first frost, and it will "bloom" once again for Christmas.

Because of its pagan associations, the use of mistletoe (left) was once forbidden by the church; because of its red blossoms at Christmastide, the Christmas cactus (right) is well-loved.

Decorating the hall all bright with holly (as immortalized by the old Welsh carol which appears on the following page) may be a familiar Christmas custom. But don't stop with just the holly; fragrant evergreens, bright berries, and cones from various trees add to the festivity.

In fashioning your holiday decorations, remember to let ingenuity be your key ingredient. Raw materials from the forest are innumerable. All but the stiffest conifer branches can be used. And although holly is time-honored wreath material, mountain laurel and ground pine (one of the club mosses) also have their admirers. Spanish moss can be employed where lacy silver-gray is desired; bittersweet berries for brightest red, and sumac hobs for a velvety scarlet. Evergreen cones, nuts, and seed pods add contrasting colors and textures.

But collect with care. Plant materials should never be removed from public lands, or from private lands without permission. Carry pruning shears or a sharp knife. Breaking branches and ripping up runners of club moss are needlessly destructive. Don't collect rare plants; and gather materials as near to Christmas as possible to prevent their drying out. If wildgrown plant materials are not available, you can usually buy conifer branches from your Christmas tree dealer or grower. Don't overlook the possibility of judiciously pruning the evergreens or holly that grow in your own backyard.

Wreaths are popular yuletide ornaments. To make a handsome one, purchase two double-wire circular frames from your florist—one 12 inches and the other 16 inches in diameter. Spiral-wrap each with a strip of 1½ or 2-inch-wide cotton cloth, overlapping the turns about ½ inch. Stuff sprigs of white pine, for example, beneath the wraps of the larger one, each group of sprigs covering the bases of the previous ones until

Two curious blue jays had their photo snapped while hunting for the peanut butter and seeds hidden in this wreath.

Greens from the Forest

Yule wreath

Miniature Christmas tree

Pinecone candleholder

the frame is entirely filled. Then do the same with the smaller frame, but using yew. Decorate the 12-inch wreath with cones, nuts, or berries, and a ribbon bow, and wire it to the face of the larger one.

Miniature Christmas "trees" are useful ornaments. Certain evergreen branches can simply be wired together to form little trees. Yew is great; white cedar's flat sprays are perfect for against-the-wall placement, and boxwood forms ultra-miniatures. The "trunk" can be set in a footed compote, saki cup, vacuum bottle cap, planter or other suitable container by means of florist putty, plaster of paris (permanent), gravel, or styrofoam. A novel idea is to push the sharpened butts of the branches into a large potato fitted into the container. The water in the potato will keep the foliage fresh. Another tree begins as a semicircle of hardware cloth rolled into a cone. Sew the edges together with wire, fill the cone with sphagnum moss, and close the large end with crisscrossed wires. Tufts of evergreen foliage are wired together and poked through the mesh until the frame is covered. Such trees will stand on saucers, inverted bowls, mirrors, etc. Decorate miniature trees with hemlock cones, berries, or tiny Christmas tree balls.

Swags are for hanging. Begin with long, graceful evergreen boughs wired together, with shorter ones covering their butts. Long cones and an assortment of other materials are wired to the evergreens, and a bow attached near the upper end.

For the wall, tack tree-shaped hardware cloth loosely to a weathered board, stuff greens into the mesh, add half a paper dish to represent a container, and trim your tree! For the table, snip the terminal scales off a flat-topped pinecone, melt wax into the resulting depression to hold a candle, and set the holder in a ring of ground pine or sphagnum moss for a lovely touch!

Ned Smith

Deck the Hall

Traditional

Old Welsh Melody

1. Deck the hall with boughs of hol - ly,
2. See the blaz - ing Yule be - fore us, } Fa, la, la, la, la, la, la, la, la.
3. Fast a - way the old year pass - es,

'Tis the sea - son to be jol - ly,
Strike the harp and join the cho - rus, } Fa, la, la, la, la, la, la, la, la.
Hail the new, ye lads and lass - es,

Don we now our gay ap - par - el,
Fol - low me in mer - ry meas - ure, } Fa, la, la, la, la, la, la, la, la.
Sing we joy - ous all to - geth - er,

Troll the an - cient Yule - tide car - ol,
While I tell of Yule - tide treas - ure, } Fa, la, la, la, la, la, la, la, la.
Heed - less of the wind and weath - er,

Burning the yule log at Christmas has its origin
in ancient winter solstice rites to rekindle the "dying" sun.

A Tree for All Seasons

Happy the man to whom every tree is a friend — who loves them, sympathizes with them in their lives in mountain and plain, in their brave struggles on barren rocks and windswept ridges, and in joyous, triumphant exuberance in fertile ravines and valleys sheltered, waving their friendly branches, while we, fondling their shining plumage, rejoice with and feel the beauty and strength of their every attitude and gesture, the swirling surging of their lifeblood in every vein and cell. Great as they are and widespread their forests over the earth's continents and islands, we may love them all and carry them about with us in our hearts. And so with the smaller flower people that dwell beneath and around them, looking up with admiring faces, or down in thoughtful poise, making all the land or garden instinct with God.

John Muir

Under a Christmas-like mantle of new-fallen snow, broad-leafed evergreens share the moist hills of Northern California with needle-bearing conifers—Douglas and other firs, and pine.

The Fir Tree

In the forest, where the warm sun and the fresh air made a sweet resting place, grew a little fir tree. The soft air fluttered its leaves, the birds sang merrily all around, and sometimes the children would come and play beside it, but it was not happy; it wished so much to be as tall as the tallest pines.

The little tree grew a notch taller every year, but as it grew it complained: "Oh, how I wish I was as tall as the other trees." Sometimes in winter, when the snow lay white on the ground, a hare would come springing along and jump right over the little tree, and then it would complain the more because it was small. Then two winters passed, and the tree became so tall that the hare had to run around it; but still it complained.

In the autumn, the woodcutters came and cut down the tallest pines, lopped off their branches and took them away. The storks told the little tree that they were to be masts for ships. "Oh, that I could be a tall mast and go to sea," sighed the fir tree. Christmas grew near, and many of the small trees were cut down and taken away.

"Where are they going?" asked the fir tree.

"We know," sang the sparrows. "We have looked into the windows of the houses in the town, and seen them dressed up splendidly, and hanging full of cakes and toys and apples, and lighted with hundreds of wax tapers." And this made the fir tree more discontented than ever.

"Rejoice with us," said the air and the sunlight.

But the tree would not rejoice. It kept longing to go to sea, or to be dressed up and lit with tapers in a warm room. A short time before Christmas, the fir tree was cut down. As it fell it could not help feeling faint, and when it thought it was leaving its companions forever, it was quite sad.

When the tree came to itself again, it discovered that it was in a yard packed with other trees. A man who was peering at it said, "This is a splendid fir tree, and we shall take it." Then two footmen in livery arrived, and they carried it off to a large and beautiful room.

How the fir tree trembled! "What is going to happen to me now?" Some young ladies came, and the servants helped them to adorn the tree. On one branch they hung little bags cut out of colored paper, and each bag was filled with sweetmeats; from other branches hung gilded apples and walnuts, as if they had grown there; and above, and all round, were hundreds of red, blue, and white tapers, which were fastened on the branches. Dolls, exactly like real babies, were placed under the green leaves —the tree had never seen such things before—and at the very top was fastened a glittering star, made of tinsel. Oh, it was very beautiful!

"This evening," they all exclaimed, "how bright it will be!" "Oh, that the evening were come," thought the tree, "and the tapers lighted! Then I shall know what else is going to happen. Will the trees of the forest come to see me? I wonder if the sparrows will peep in at the windows as they fly? Shall I grow faster here, and keep on all these ornaments during summer and winter?" At last the tapers were lighted, and then what a glistening blaze of light the tree presented! The tree quivered so much in all its splendor that one of the tapers fell and singed a branch. "Take care," cried one of the young ladies who had helped in the decorating. When the taper was again set upright the tree did not dare to move.

And then the folding doors were thrown open, and a troop of children rushed in. They shouted for joy till the room rang, and they danced merrily round the tree, while one present after another was taken from it.

"What are they doing? What will happen next?" thought the fir. At last the candles burnt down to the branches and were put out. Then the children received permission to plunder the tree.

Oh, how they rushed upon it, till the branches cracked; and had it not been fastened with the glistening star to the ceiling, it might have fallen. The children then danced about with their pretty toys. No one noticed the tree except the children's maid, who came and peeped among the branches to see if an apple or a fig had been forgotten, perhaps.

The children, having plundered the tree, now decided that they wished to hear a story. Pulling a roly-poly looking man into the room, they begged, "A story, uncle. Please tell us a story!"

"It will be my pleasure," said the uncle. "But we have only enough time to hear about Humpty Dumpty before you must go to bed."

The children grew quiet, and sat themselves down on the floor about the tree to listen. Then the old man told them of Humpty Dumpty who fell down the stairs, but was raised up and married a princess. All the children thought that this was a fine story, and so did the fir tree.

In the morning the servants and the housemaid came in. "Now," thought the fir, "all my splendor is going to begin again." But instead they dragged it out of the room and upstairs to the garret. There they threw it on the floor, in a dark corner, where no daylight shone. And there they left it.

Yearning to be tall enough to be sent to sea as a mast, the tiny fir tree took no joy in the birds that sang in its branches nor in the hares who leapt over it; by the end of the third season, the hares had to hop around the "big" little tree, and the tree rejoiced.

"What does this mean?" thought the tree. "What am I to do here? I can hear nothing in a place like this." It leant against the wall, and thought and thought. And it had time enough to think, for days and nights passed and no one came near it. When at last somebody did come, it was only to put away large boxes in a corner. So the tree was completely hidden from sight, as if it had never existed.

"It is winter now in the forest," thought the tree; "the ground is hard and covered with snow, so that people cannot plant me. I shall be sheltered here, I dare say, until spring comes. How thoughtful and kind everybody is to me! Still I wish this place were not so dark, as well as lonely, with not even a little hare to look at. How pleasant it was out in the forest while the snow lay on the ground, when the hare would run by. Yes, and jump over me, too, although I did not like it then. Oh! it is terribly lonely here."

"Squeak, squeak!" said a little mouse who crept out of a hole in the floorboards to investigate the tree. As it sniffed the branches it was joined by another mouse.

"It's terribly cold in here," squeaked the two mice in unison. "Don't you think so, old fir tree?"

"Why, I'm not old at all," said the tree. "There are many in the forest who are older and taller than myself."

"Tell us about the forest," said the mice. "Is it as nice as the storeroom where the bacon and cheese hang from the ceiling?"

"I don't know about that," said the tree. "But I do know about the woods and sunshine, and birds which sing." And the tree told of its youth in the forest.

The little mice, who had lived only in the house, were spellbound. "What a great number of things you have seen," they said. "How happy you must have been."

"Me?" replied the tree. And then it thought about all that it had told the mice. "Yes," it said quietly. "Those really were happy times. But the happiest moment in my life was the night I became a Christmas tree." And it described to them the moment in the great room when the doors were thrown open and all the children rushed in and exclaimed at the beautiful tree. It told of the father who lifted the baby up in his arms to see the star on its crown; and of all the gaily wrapped toys which were carefully arranged around its base, and of the children's excitement as they stood around the tree eagerly awaiting the chance to find their presents.

The next day when the mice came to visit they brought a great many more mice with them. "Tell us of the forest and how you became a Christmas tree," they all cried.

And so once again the tree began to tell of its earlier life outdoors, and of its one splendid night in the great room downstairs. The mice were very pleased with the story, and to show their appreciation they leapt to the top of the fir's branches and scrambled down with pleasure.

On Sunday when the mice came again they were accompanied by two rats. But the rats were not at all impressed with the story; and their disapproval caused the mice not to like the tale so much as before.

"Do you know only that one story?" inquired the rats.

The fir tree thought a moment—remembering all that it had heard on Christmas Eve—and then asked, "Would you like to know of Humpty Dumpty?"

"Who is Humpty Dumpty?" the little mice asked.

So then the tree related the whole story, just as the jolly uncle had told it.

At first all the mice were delighted with the adventure. But the two rats declared that they still weren't satisfied.

"That's a very miserable story," they said. "Don't you know anything about bacon and cheese?"

"No," said the tree.

"Then we'd rather not listen," wheezed the rats as they waddled away. All the little mice followed, and they did not return the following morning.

One day the tree was dragged out of the garret and thrown in the yard. By this time, its branches were yellow and withered. "Now," it thought, "I only hope they will think to take me back to the forest."

Alas, a servant soon came and cut the tree into little bits, and it was thrown on the fire to make the kettle boil. The branches sighed deeply, and every sigh rang out like a shot. The children soon left their play and came to sit down before the fire, looking into it, and crying out, "Puff! Puff!"

As the fire crept around the branches, one of the youngsters spied the glittering star which the tree had worn on the happiest evening of its life. Snatching it, the boy pinned it to the breast of his jacket and paraded happily around the garden. Now that has passed away—and the tree has passed away—and the story has ended.

Adapted from
Hans Christian
Andersen

Choosing a Christmas Tree

O ur most enchanting holiday custom, the evergreen tree for Christmas, is so new that only 100 years ago Charles Dickens was calling it "a pretty German toy," yet it is so old that its birth becomes lost in antiquity. In ancient Rome, small, decorated trees and evergreens were prominent in most winter solstice ceremonies. The Germans were the first Europeans to accept the Christmas tree fashion widely, and in the 16th century they were decorating trees with stars, bells, flowers, and other symbols.

By the late 1700s, the Christmas tree had spread throughout the continent. At about that time, it was also brought to this country, folklore says, by Hessian soldiers hired to fight against George Washington in the American Revolution. About a half century later, the seal of approval was stamped on the Christmas tree in England when Queen Victoria and her German-born husband, Prince Albert, put up a tree at Windsor Castle.

Whether you choose to cut your own—as this New England youngster did—or buy from a lot, your Christmas tree choice is varied. For easy identification, eight evergreen favorites are shown on pages 150-151.

In the early part of this century, President Theodore Roosevelt became alarmed that the tree custom might mean that American forests would be depleted. He banned all trees from the White House festivities, but then discovered that two of his sons had smuggled an evergreen into their room. With the friendly intervention of Gifford Pinchot—the nation's first professional forester—Roosevelt was won over to the precedent that selective cutting was actually helpful to forest growth. The Roosevelt boys kept their tree, and the White House has had an indoor Christmas tree ever since.

There is no "best" evergreen for a Christmas tree. The correct choice depends on each individual's taste in shape, color, and scent. Pines and firs hold their needles best; but properly cared for, spruces keep well for 10 to 12 days. If a living Christmas tree is preferred—a potted tree which can be planted later—a variety should be chosen that is well suited to the area in which it is going to be grown.

Christmas trees—like trees everywhere—have stories to tell. For example, a tree's age may be revealed by examining the rings at the cut end. Each ring represents a year's growth. A tree's rings may tell other things besides age, however. For example, if the rings are wide near the center of the stem and then get narrow towards the bark, the tree might have grown in a Christmas tree plantation. As the trees around it grew, they crowded this particular tree so that it grew less each year. It might also mean there was not enough rain. Or perhaps the soil was losing its fertility. If the rings get wider near the bark, that could mean growing conditions improved.

After Christmas, give your discarded tree new meaning and new life. Redecorate it with strings of popcorn and cranberries, or suet bags, as an outside feeder, or group your tree with others on the ground so that their inner branches touch. Small mammals and birds will use this brush pile as a protected hiding place, as well as a shelter from winter storms. If you plan well, your Christmas tree will not only bring nature to your home but, in the true yuletide spirit, continue the gift-giving throughout the year.

Scotch pine
Imported from Europe and widely planted in North America, this pine's needles are stiff, yellow-green 1.5—3 inches long, in bundles of two. Trunk often crooked, grows to 50 feet.

Douglas fir
An important timber tree, its long clear trunk grows rapidly to 250 feet in moist Pacific Coast area. Needles, 1—1.5 inches long, stick out in all directions from branches.

Balsam fir
Growing throughout eastern Canada, the Balsam fir's needles are flat, .8—1.5 inches long, usually notched at the tip. It reaches 40—60 feet tall and 1—1.5 feet in diameter.

Eastern red cedar
Found throughout the eastern half of the country, this tree grows best in limestone regions. It has a dense pyramidal crown and becomes 40—50 feet tall and 1—2 feet in diameter.

Black spruce
Needles are dark
green and .5 of an
inch long. Cones, up
to 1 inch long, are
brittle and often hang
on trees for years.
Black spruce grow
throughout Canada
and reach 30—
40 feet.

Red pine
Found in northeastern
U.S. and southeastern
Canada, this species
grows 50—100
feet tall. Needles are
4—6 inches long.
Though native
American, the Red
pine is also called
Norway pine.

White pine
This largest conifer
in the Northeast grows
75—100 feet tall
and 2—4 feet
in diameter. It has a
pyramidal crown of
whorled horizontal
branches. Needles are
3—5 inches long
in bundles of 5.

Norway spruce
Imported from Europe,
many varieties of
Norway spruce are
planted in the U.S.
and Canada. It grows
125 feet tall. Needles
are dark green,
.5—.8 of an inch
long, flattened to
triangular.

Critters in the Branches

The animals you enjoy most can decorate your Christmas tree, and you can have fun making them. In a large bowl, mix 4 cups of unsifted flour, 1 cup of salt, and 1 to 1½ cups of water. Knead the clay four to five minutes. If it's too stiff add just a little water. (Caution: Do NOT double the recipe or cut it in half—the clay will not be workable.) Lay the animals on a cookie sheet and use bottle tops, forks, toothpicks, popsicle or lollipop sticks to press in designs. When adding legs or ears, moisten them so that they will stick. And don't forget to provide a hook for hanging the figures. A hairpin, piece of wire, or a paper clip pushed firmly into the clay before baking will serve the purpose well.

Preheat the oven to 350°F. and bake the figures for one hour—longer if they are soft. Spread them out to cool; use poster paints, felt tip markers, beads, and glue to decorate; and spray with a clear fixative to preserve. This recipe makes about 6 to 8 figures. But remember, even though these critters look good enough to eat, they are just for show.

To make animals from cardboard, colored paper, and scraps of felt, find pictures you like and trace the outlines on tissue paper. Glue the designs onto cardboard, trim the edges, and paste on fabric or colored paper. Add sequins, bright yarn, and pipe cleaners—including ones to serve as hooks—and you will have a host of perky friends ready to peek out from the branches of your Christmas tree.

Fashioned from clay—and hung in suspended animation—these whimsical creatures of field, stream, and wood add an extra touch of "life" to the tree.

153

The red fox, a frequent visitor near the author's lodge in central Ontario, looks chubby. Don't be deceived. Winter fur disguises a slender frame—easily encircled by a man's thumb and forefinger.

I remember the night of the fox.
The violence of winter
*   lay on the land.*
I went out for another log
And the night captured me.
The air was still.
*   Sere bur oak leaves*
Spotted the crusty snow.
In the silver-blue silence
*   I was alone*
In the universe.

All my memories were as distant hills.
Then out of the north
The violet Aurora flailed the skies
Streaking and screaming
Staining the crusty snow
In a cold fury.
The silence bit my soul.
No wind stirred.
The vapors of my breath
*   the only motion.*

At Wildlife's Door

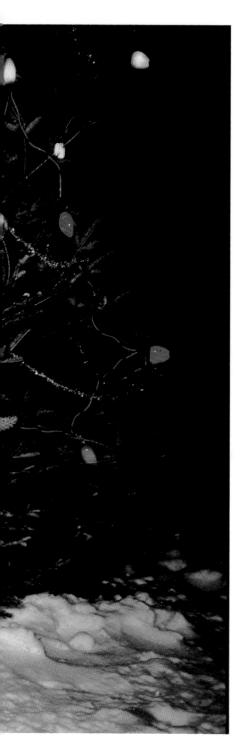

I live in Northern Algonquin Park, a 3,000 square-mile primitive area set aside in 1893 as a recreation zone and wildlife preserve in the central part of the Province of Ontario.

In the summer of 1927, my Mother, Dad, and I built a lodge. Kish Kaduk we call it after the Algonquin for Cedar Lake, near which it stands. Our nearest town is 58 miles away by railroad. Because we have no roads into our place, and because the area is a game preserve, wildlife friends are numerous.

Our winter starts in about the third week of October, and ends around the first of May when the ice leaves the lakes. During this time we are visited by many of the wild creatures of the forest around us.

There are no hydroelectric power lines in our part of the park, so we generate our own electricity. During the Christmas season we become a bit frivolous and waste some of our power on a decorated tree in the front yard. We do not consider the tree lights a waste of power because there is no way one can measure the great amount of pleasure we receive from the visits of the animals to our yard and around our tree.

The most frequent visitors are deer, foxes, raccoons, marten, and sometimes mink. We also see wolves out on the lake ice at times during the day, and there are quite a number of moose around us, but they are aloof animals, and prefer the solitude of the bush farther from the house, though they do tramp through our hard-earned vegetable garden from time to time.

All of the animals are wild and free. We do try to make friends of them by feeding them tidbits, but we are careful not to give them too much of anything so as not to upset their natural food balance. We save the excess fat from all of our roasts and fries in the kitchen, and this we spread like butter on pieces of bread for treats for the foxes, raccoons and marten. They apparently consider the fat a great delicacy, because they soon become very friendly and come to us to be hand fed. The deer like cedar browse that we collect and put around the yard for them, and the mink enjoy meat scraps.

The fox in the photograph was a frequent visitor, and would stop to be photographed if one was quick enough on the shutter and emitted a few squeaks to get his attention.

Rose Thomas

Sparks from my chimney top
Were bright among the stars
Against the deep blue night.
I was frozen in the night.
Frozen in time and space.
Frozen beside the great bur oak.
Part of time.
Part of the beginning and the end.
Part of eternity.

Like the crack of doom
The great bur oak
Was rent
By her frozen sap
And her massive limbs
Lay black on the crusty snow.
It was as though death
*   stalked the earth*
In violet robes.
Then I saw the fox.

In the violet silence we stood
And each looked into
*   the other's eyes*
And shared the universe
In a strange communion.
Then in a spurt he was gone.
I carried another log to my fire.
This was the night of the fox.

Gouverneur Smith

As Christmas draws near, Thoreau's advice—simplify, get down to the essentials—releases the memory of the year we simplified Christmas. Time rushes back—and I live it again. . . .

There we were at the turn of the forest path, weighed down with fresh-cut holly and fir boughs powdered with snow. The children, carrying greens, raced ahead to the clearing, their laughter flung back to us like silver darts. Everything in the forest was silver that afternoon before Christmas Eve: trees all silver-dusted, the trail glittering in a frozen shaft of sunlight that cheered but did little to warm us. The air was clear, stinging cold. Breathing was like inhaling silver icicles.

Long before we reached the cabin the children were there, rolling great snowballs for a snowman they were building beside the door. Their shouts followed us in-side and punctuated our preparations for supper and the evening's festivities. By sundown, the snowman stood sentinel at the doorstep, jaunty in red hunting jacket and cap, and the children piled into the cabin hungry as bears. Winter twilight came slowly and settled in the clearing.

A wilderness Christmas Eve—how to describe the beauty of it? The cabin, the clearing, the whole forest radiant in the light of a million stars . . . frosted trees standing silent, infinitely majestic at the clearing's edge . . . rabbit tracks crisscrossing the path and disappearing into the dark of the woods . . . sheaves of grain and suet strings, hung on low branches for the birds' Christmas feast, glazing in the icy wind . . . and high in the eastern sky, a thin slice of winter moon. It was a Christmas card scene, almost unreal.

Inside, the cabin was transformed with fir boughs and holly piled on the mantle and framing the windows,

"Morning" from a Currier and Ives American winter scene.

to Remember

mistletoe tied above the door, a crèche and candles on the table, stockings hung at the chimney, and simple gifts from the nearest village variety store piled beside the hearth, to be opened in the morning. Supper was by candlelight, a jolly meal soon finished and cleared away. Then there were games, forfeits, and general hilarity that rocked the cabin and threatened to burst the walls. But quiet came after a while when the children, tiring of games, begged for stories and we gathered before the crackling fire, passing around great bowls of apples, nuts and raisins. The moan of an owl from somewhere nearby gave eerie accompaniment to our ghostly fire. And at length, just before bedtime, the sleepy children climbed on our laps and listened to the Christmas story, joining in carols sung softly as the candles and the fire burned low.

Then we all trooped outside for a look at the midnight sky; and there, at the edge of the clearing, two deer raised their heads to stare, immobile in the starlight. We were spellbound. It was a moment from that first Christmas Eve, suspended in time. The stars looked down, the beasts stood by, and there was deep peace on the land. But only for a moment. Clapping her hands ecstatically, the youngest child cried, "It's Donner and Blitzen!" Breaking the spell, she sped the animals on their way. Everyone went off to bed, leaving the night's vigil to the moon and stars.

We won't be spending Christmas at the wilderness cabin this year. We will be right here at home. But one thing is certain: we are going to simplify. . . . And we will come to Christmas morning serene, unwearied, and with good will in our hearts.

Mary Wilson

When the ponds were firmly frozen, they afforded not only new and shorter routes to many points, but new views from their surfaces of the familiar landscape around them.

When I crossed Flints Pond, after it was covered with snow, though I had often paddled about and skated over it, it was so unexpectedly wide and so strange that I could think of nothing but Baffin's Bay. The Lincoln hills rose up around me at the extremity of a snowy plain, in which I did not remember to have stood before; and the fishermen, at an indeterminable distance over the ice, moving slowly about with their wolfish dogs, passed for sealers or Esquimaux, or in misty weather loomed like fabulous creatures, and I did not know whether they were giants or pygmies.

Henry David Thoreau

TEXT CREDITS

The Editors wish to acknowledge appreciation to publishers for permission to present the following selections:

"Ark Full of Cookies, An" (p. 69), Noah's Ark Recipes. Reprinted by permission of McCall's, December 1973 issue of *McCall's Magazine*.

"Birds in Winter" (p. 103), by Walter de la Mare from *The Burning-Glass and Other Poems*, by permission of The Literary Trustees of Walter de la Mare, and The Society of Authors as their representative.

"Four Paintings by the Artist" (p. 24), an excerpt from "The Colloid and the Crystal", Chapter 11; and "Frost Flowers" (p. 28), an excerpt from "Making the Days Seem Long", Chapter 10—both reprinted from Joseph Wood Krutch, *The Best of Two Worlds,* by permission of the copyright owners, The Trustees of Columbia University in the City of New York.

Jean George articles copyright 1962 & 1966—Reader's Digest Association, Inc.

"Legend of the Mountain Goat, The" (p. 68), originally published as "The Mountain Goat" adapted from *Raven-Who-Sets-Things-Right*, Indian Tales of the Northwest Coast Retold by Fran Martin. Text copyright © 1975 by Frances McEntee Martin. Reprinted by permission of Harper & Row, Publishers, Inc.

"Living Ornaments" (p. 134), an essay originally entitled "The Festive Berries" abridged from *Borland Country* by Hal Borland. Copyright © 1971, 1956, 1955, 1953, 1952, 1951, 1950, 1949, 1948, 1947. Reprinted by permission of J. B. Lippincott Company.

"Night Before Christmas, The" (p. 78), by Clement Clarke Moore, originally entitled "A Visit from Saint Nicholas", courtesy of the Manuscript Department, The New York-Historical Society.

"65290" (p. 126), an excerpt from *A Sand County Almanac with other essays on conservation from Round River* by Aldo Leopold. Copyright © 1949, 1953, 1966 by Oxford University Press, Inc. Reprinted by permission.

"Snow Fun" (p. 39), instructions for making colored icicles, adapted from booklet published by Minnesota Environmental Sciences Foundation, Inc.

Snow Maiden, The (p. 40), courtesy of The Copyright Agency of the USSR (VAAP).

"Some Creatures Were Stirring" (p. 80), excerpt from chapter entitled "Dulce Domum". Reprinted by permission of Charles Scribner's Sons from *The Wind in the Willows* by Kenneth Grahame, illustrations by Ernest H. Shepard. Illustrations copyright © 1960 Ernest H. Shepard. Text copyright 1908 Charles Scribner's Sons. British Commonwealth Rights: Methuen Children's Books Ltd., London, England; Text Copyright University Chest Oxford.

"Tree for All Seasons, A" (p. 142), excerpt from *John of the Mountains: The Unpublished Journals of John Muir*, edited by L. M. Wolfe; Houghton Mifflin, 1938.

"Who Killed Cock Robin?" (p. 128), excerpt from "A Fable for Tomorrow", in *Silent Spring*, Rachel Carson. Copyright © 1962 by Rachel L. Carson. Reprinted by permission of Houghton Mifflin Company and by permission of the Estate of the Author.

"Year Santa Came Late, The" (p. 82), originally published as "The Strategy of the Were-Wolf Dog". Abridged by permission from *Willa Cather's Collected Short Fiction, 1892-1912* (revised edition). Edited by Virginia Faulkner. Introduction by Mildred R. Bennett. Copyright © 1965, 1970 by the University of Nebraska Press.

PICTURE CREDITS

Cover: Cardinal on Possum Haw, Thase Daniel. Page 1: Evergreens and Pinecones, Joseph Van Wormer. 2-3: Three Deer in Snow, Norman Lightfoot/Photo Researchers. 5: Poinsettias, Grant Heilman. 6-7: Mt. Hood and Lost Lake, Oregon, Ray Atkeson.

DECEMBER DAYS

Pages 8-9: Creek in Colorado Rockies, David Muench. 10-11: Castle Rock, Oak Creek Canyon, Arizona, Ray Manley from Shostal. 12-13: Canada Geese in Massachusetts, Arthur Griffin. 14-15: Table Mountain in Mt. Baker National Forest, Washington, Ray Atkeson. 16: Snow Geese at Pea Island, N.C., Grant Heilman. 17: White-tailed Deer Along Lake Superior, Minnesota, Les Blacklock. 18-19: Currier and His Wife—"The Road-Winter", Currier and Ives, The Harry T. Peters Collection, Museum of the City of New York. 20-21: "Jingle Bells", James Pierpont. 23: Snow on Fallen Tree, Arnout Hyde, Jr. 24-27: Tree in Winter/Spring/Summer/Fall, Walter Dawn. 28: Frost on Pane, Grant Heilman. 30-31: Clockwise: Frost on Grass, Red Berries, Leaves, Bird's Nest; all by Larry West; Queen Anne's Lace, Robert O. Joslin. 32: Clockwise: Ice on Blue Spruce Cone, Weeds, Poverty Grass, Milkweed Pod, Catkins and Leaf of the White Birch; Ruth H. Smiley, and Robert K. Hoffman. 33: Left to right: Ice on Pine Mohonk, Blades of Grass, Cattails, Cranberry Viburnum, and Pitch Pine; Larry West and Ruth H. Smiley. 34-35: Snowflakes, P. J. Hoff; Yosemite in Winter, David Muench. 36-37: Icicles, Tom Myers. 38: Tufted Titmouse, William D. Griffin. 39: Snow Fun, Top: Drawing by Joan Orfe. Bottom: Drawings, both by James Reid. 40-43: *The Snow Maiden* art—Ms. Eremina, VAAP, Moscow, USSR.

WILDLIFE IN WINTER

Pages 44-45: Raccoon, Leonard Lee Rue III. 46: Top: Otter on Snow Bank; Bottom left: Otter Sliding; Bottom right: Otter Eating Snowballs; all by John L. Ebeling. 47: Squirrel, Larry West. 48: Meadowlark, Jack Dermid. 50: Chipmunk, Lynwood M. Chace. 51: Fox, Dr. G.J. Chafaris. 52: Deer, Leonard Lee Rue III. 53: Deer ("We Three Kings") Harry J. Moeller. 54: Song Sparrow, William D. Griffin. 54-55: Ruffed Grouse, "Snowed Up", Currier and Ives, The Harry T. Peters Collection, Museum of the City of New York. 55: Varying Hare, Leonard Lee Rue III. 57: Left: Coyote, John S. Crawford. Right: Red Fox Tracks, Gabe Cherem. 58-59: Left: Two Branches, Davis Meltzer. Bottom left: Footprints in Snow, Karl H. Maslowski. Right: Cottontail, Karl H. Maslowski. 60-61: Top: Tracks in Snow, Arthur Anderson. Bottom left to right: Opossum, Allan Roberts; Cottontail Rabbit, Dan McPeek; Fox, Wilford Miller; Mouse, Larry West; Gray Squirrel, Leonard Lee Rue III; Raccoon, Laura Riley; Longtail Weasel, Ray Noyes. 62: Mother Bear and Cubs, Lynn Rogers. 63: Left and right: Moose, both by Erwin A. Bauer. 64: Bison, ENTHEOS. 65: Bull Elk, Les Blacklock. 66-67: Top: Arctic Fox © Walt Disney Productions; Bottom, left to right: Least Weasel, Karl H. Maslowski; Wolves, Patricia Caulfield; Snowshoe Rabbit, Leonard Lee Rue III. 68: Riggs Glacier, Keith Gunnar. 69: Mountain Goat Kid, Leonard Lee Rue III. 70-71: Mountain Goat, Erwin A. Bauer. 73: Left and right: Totem Poles, both by Alexander K. Ciesielski. 74: Tundra Reindeer, Fred Baldwin. 75: Caribou, Nicholas deVore III/Bruce Coleman, Inc. 76: Wooden Santa Figure by Charles Robb, Abby Aldrich Rockefeller Folk Art Collection. 76-77: "City of New York from Jersey City", Currier & Ives, The Harry T. Peters Collection, Museum of the City of New York. 79: Thomas Nast Cartoon from *Harpers Weekly*, The Granger Collection, New York. 80 and 81: Mice Visiting Mole

End, both Reprinted by permission of Charles Scribner's Sons from *The Wind in The Willows* by Kenneth Grahame, illustrations by Ernest H. Shepard. Illustrations copyright © 1960 Ernest H. Shepard. Text copyright 1908 Charles Scribner's Sons. 83: Aurora Borealis, Gustav Lamprecht. 84: Wolf, Patricia Caulfield, ANIMALS ANIMALS. 86-87: Reindeer, Steven C. Wilson from D.P.I. 88-89: Polar Bear, Lee Miller/Photo Researchers. 90: Lapp Boy and Reindeer, Bob and Ira Spring. 90-91: Caribou, Bill Staender. 92: Map—Caribou Lands, Vincent Piecyk. 93: Caribou ENTHEOS. 94-95: *Noah's Ark*, painting by Edward Hicks, Philadelphia Museum of Art: Bequest of Lisa Norris Elkins. 96-97: Ark and Cookies, Irwin Horowitz (December 1973 issue of *McCall's*) Reprinted by McCall's Permission. 98: Pattern for Gingerbread Ark, (December 1973 issue of *McCall's*) Reprinted by McCall's Permission. 99: Stained Glass, Al Cassuto. 100-101: Carol "The Friendly Beasts" — including art work (pp. 106-107) in A BOOK OF CHRISTMAS CAROLS, Selected and Illustrated by Haig and Regina Shekerjian. Arranged for Piano, with Guitar Chords by Robert De Cormier. Copyright © 1963 by Haig and Regina Shekerjian. By Permission of Harper and Row, Publishers, Inc., and British Rights courtesy of Arthur Barker Ltd.

THE BIRDS OF CHRISTMAS

102-103: Mockingbird, Thase Daniel. 104-105: Egrets, Mike Shea. 107: Great Horned Owl, Wilbur S. Tripp. 108-109: Left: Pileated Woodpecker, Perry Covington/Tom Stack & Associates. Top right: Goshawk, Dr. E. R. Degginger. Bottom right: Pine Grosbeak, Winston Pote. 110: Top: Indigo Buntings; left, Fall and Winter; right, Spring and Summer, John Tveten. Bottom: Rose-breasted Grosbeak, Russ Kinne. 111: Left: Baltimore (Northern) Oriole, Ron Austing. Right: Purple Martin, Lula Dorman. 112: Ruffed Grouse, Dan McPeek. 113: Bobwhite, Ron Klataske. 114-115: Adaptation of the Art, "Partridge in a Pear Tree", from *The Twelve Days of Christmas; a Picture Book*, Robert Broomfield © Bodley Head Ltd. Carol, Frederick Austin arrangement, © 1956 Novella & Co. Ltd., used by Permission. 116-117: Puffin, Ruth H. Smiley. 118: Junco, Dan McPeek. 120-121: Mallards, Erwin A. Bauer. 123: Top: Evening Grosbeaks on Feeder, Mrs. Pearl E. Paquette. Bottom: Downy Woodpecker, George H. Harrison. 124: Top: Goldfinches on Swedish Christmas Tree; Bottom: Cardinal on Feeder; both by George H. Harrison. 125: Left: Chickadee on String of Doughnuts, Richard B. Fischer. Right: Pygmy Nuthatch on Pinecone Feeder, Kent and Donna Dannen. 126: Chickadee on Pinecone, William D. Griffin. 129: "The Death and Burial of Cock Robin" by J. B. Zwecker, from *Mother Goose Melodies Set to Music*, designed under superintendence of and engraved by The Brothers Dalziel © 1872. 130-131: Christmas Cards, Hallmark Historical Collection.

DECK THE HALLS FOR ONE AND ALL

132-133: Mouse on Christmas Tree, Alvin E. Staffan. 135: Left: Holly; Right: Poinsettias; both by Grant Heilman. 136: Mistletoe, Jack Dermid. 137: Christmas Cactus, Stephen Beck. 138: Blue Jays on Wreath, Russ Kinne. 139: Line Art, Ned Smith. 140: "Deck the Hall with Boughs of Holly", and 141: Print ("See the Blazing Yule Before Us") by F. D. Lohman, from *Christmas Carols*, copyright 1938, copyright renewed 1966 by Western Publishing Company, Inc. reprinted by permission. 142-143: Winter in Northern California, Ed Cooper Photo. 144: Birds, and 145: Top: Trees; Bottom: Rabbits and Fir Tree by Hans Tegner, prints from Hans Christian Andersen's *Fairy Tales* © 1900, Library of Congress Rare Book Room. 146: Top: Noah's Ark Toy, Abby Aldrich Rockefeller Folk Art Collection. Bottom: Teddy Bear, Smithsonian Institution, Gift of Col. Theodore Barnes. 147: Print (Family gathered around Christmas Tree) from Hans Christian Andersen's *Fairy Tales* (1900), Library of Congress Rare Book Room. 148-149: Top: Youth with Christmas Tree, Winston Pote from Shostal. 150-151: Evergreen Trees, Ralph Winter. 152-153: Ornaments made by Marian Ebert—Photographed by Gisela Jordan. 154-155: Red Fox beside Christmas Tree, Rose Thomas. 156: "American Winter Scenes — Morning", Currier and Ives, The Harry T. Peters Collection, Museum of the City of New York.

ILLUSTRATORS

Broomfield, Robert, "Partridge in a Pear Tree", contemporary British author and illustrator of children's books.

Currier and Ives, N. Currier, 19th century American printmaker and lithographer later joined by James Meritt Ives.

Ms. Eremina, Russian artist in Moscow selected to illustrate *The Snow Maiden*.

Hicks, Edward (1780-1849), *Noah's Ark*, (1846), Quaker preacher, coach and sign painter known for his folk art and especially for his many versions of "The Peaceable Kingdom".

Moeller, Harry J., Three deer, "Christmas Star". Contemporary natural history illustrator.

Nast, Thomas (1840-1902), " 'Twas the Night Before Christmas". American political cartoonist, born in Germany, known especially for his attacks on New York's Tammany Hall in 1870.

Prang, Louis (1824-1909), German-born lithographer, wood engraver, issued color reproductions of famous paintings.

Robb, Charles, 19th century wooden Santa Claus used for display, from the Abby Aldrich Rockefeller folk art collection in Williamsburg.

Shekerjian, Regina, "The Friendly Beasts", contemporary American artist.

Shepard, Ernest, "Mole End", English artist and cartoonist best known for illustrating *Winnie the Pooh* and *The Wind in the Willows*.

Tegner, Hans Christian Harold (1853-1932), "The Fir Tree," award-winning Danish painter, designer, illustrator.

Zwecker, Johann Baptist (1815-1876), "Death and Burial of Cock Robin", illustrator of books in Germany and England.

Illustrations by the following artists are reprinted in this book from National Wildlife Federation magazines: Anderson, Arthur, "Animal Tracks". Meltzer, Davis, Line drawing of branches. Orfe, Joan, Drawing of "Snow Fun" activity (top of page). Piecyk, Vincent, Caribou Lands Range Map, Contemporary American artist. Reid, James, Drawings of several "Snow Fun" activities (bottom of page). Winter, Ralph, Child and father choosing Christmas tree.

Library of Congress Cataloging in Publication Data

Main entry under title:

Wildlife's Christmas treasury.

1. Nature—Literary collections. 2. Christmas—Literary collections. 3. Winter—Literary collections. I. National Wildlife Federation.
PN6071.N3W5   808.8'033   76-12388
ISBN 0-912186-22-4

National Wildlife Federation

1412 16th Street, N.W.
Washington, D.C. 20036

Thomas L. Kimball, Executive Vice President
J. A. Brownridge, Administrative Vice President
James D. Davis, Director, Book Development

Staff for this Book

Natalie S. Rifkin, Editor
Patricia G. Towle, Writer-Researcher
Ellen R. Balderson, Editorial Secretary
Leah Bendavid-Val, Permissions Editor
Mel Baughman, Production and Printing

Acknowledgments

The editor and staff feel fortunate to have had Charles O. Hyman, who designed *Gardening With Wildlife* (NWF © 1974) and *History of Wildlife in America* (NWF © 1975), work with us on the design of *Wildlife's Christmas Treasury*.

To the many persons at National Wildlife Federation who have been instrumental in the preparation of this book, we owe our appreciation also:

Tina Bandle, Janice Hawkins, and Jack Shepherd—Production Artists;
Bernard Featherson—Production Photographer
Robert C. Glotzhober, Naturalist, and Craig Tufts, Asst. Naturalist,
for their verification of natural history information.
William E. Clark, Jennifer Connor, and Alma Deane MacConomy
for their editorial proofing.
Gail Axtell, Lorraine Crowe, Margaret Egan, Virginia Howe, Barbara
Langston, Janet Lomauro, Fran Mitchell, Kittie Rothschild, Sandy
Tart, and Vivien Witheford for their manuscript typing.

We are grateful to the editors of *National Wildlife, International Wildlife,* and *Ranger Rick's Nature Magazine* for their cooperation.

Special thanks are also due the personnel at the research facilities of the Fairfax County Public Library; U.S. Fish and Wildlife Service; U.S. Forest Service; U.S. Geological Survey; Library of Congress; Patuxent Wildlife Research Center; and the Smithsonian Institution.

And finally, the editor and staff wish to thank the following individuals for their generous assistance: David McC. Grubb, Linguistics Dept., University of Victoria, British Columbia; Julia E. Harty, Rare Book and Special Collections Division, Library of Congress; William Howarth, Firestone Library, Princeton University; Dr. Badim Medish, Professor of Russian Studies, American University; Dr. and Mrs. Lev N. Mitrokhin, Embassy of the U.S.S.R.; Chandler S. Robbins, Migratory Bird and Habitat Research Lab, U.S. Fish and Wildlife Service, Laurel, Md.; Rodris Roth, Curator of Costume and Furnishing, Smithsonian Institution; Dr. Ronald Skoog, Chief, Office of Endangered Species, U.S. Fish and Wildlife Service; and Gordon Correll Vaeth, student, American University, translator of the Russian folktale, *The Snow Maiden*.